BIRDIES, BOGEYS, AND BELLY LAUGHS

"Birdies, Bogeys, and Belly Laughs" immerses readers in the universal struggles and triumphs of golf, offering a sanctuary for those navigating the unpredictable course. Through witty tales, relatable misadventures, and insights into the pursuit of golf, it unveils the transformative power of humor and shared experiences, inspiring a renewed passion for the game.

Max Fielder

TABLE OF CONTENTS

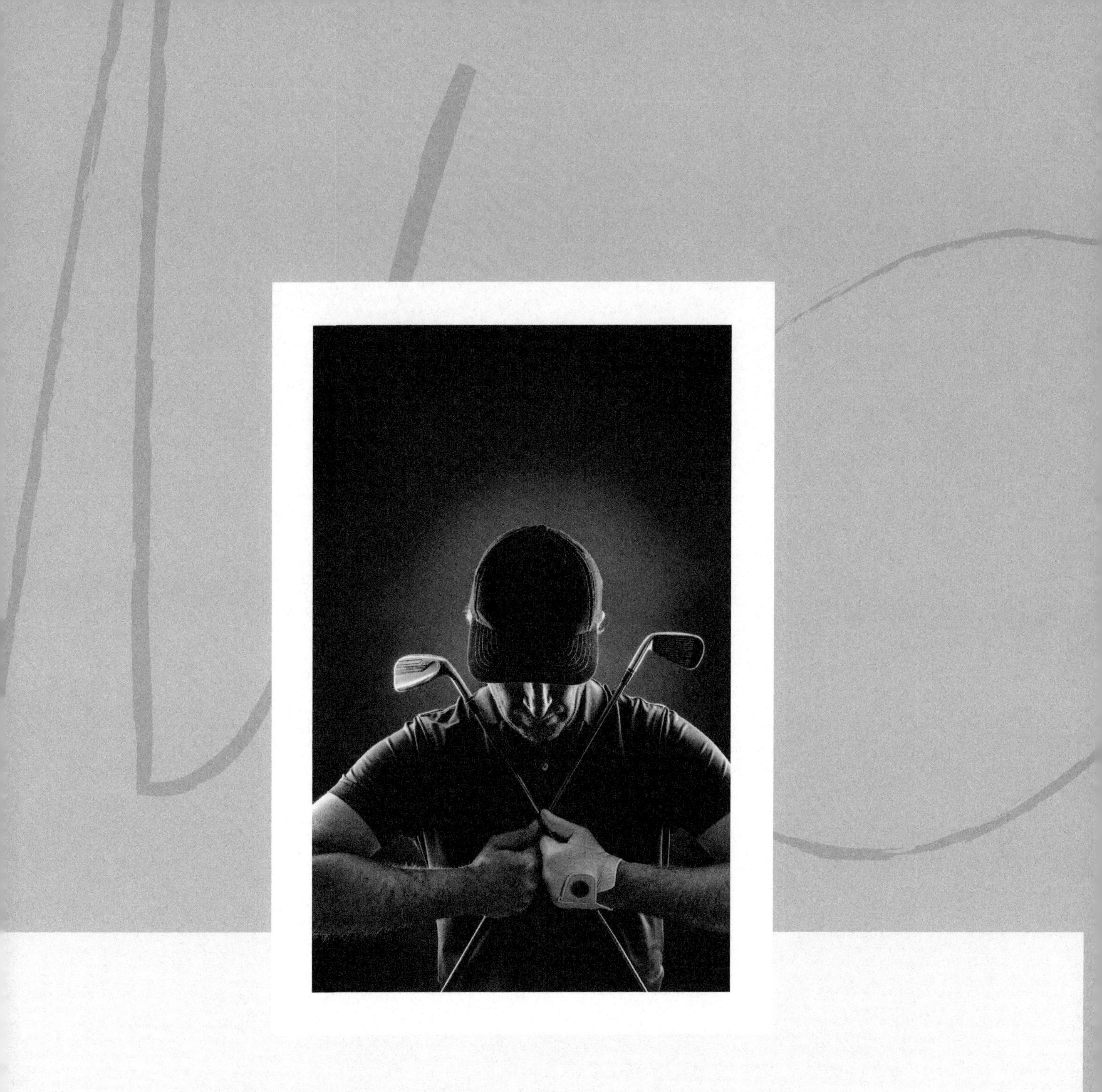

“I always think under par. You have to believe in yourself.”

SERGIO GARCIA

Introduction

In the vast expanse of the golfing world, where fairways stretch endlessly and the exhilaration of a perfect swing collides with the exasperation of missed putts, one common bond ties golfers of every skill level together: an unyielding determination to master this enigmatic game. This pursuit simultaneously fuels passion and frustration, orchestrating a delicate ballet between ambition and reality. And for those of us ensnared in the tumultuous whirlwind of vexation, seeking refuge amidst the triumphs and trials of the course, "Birdies, Bogeys, and Belly Laughs" presents a glimmer of optimism and a thoroughly earned dose of mirth.

Envision, if you will, the familiar narrative of a mid-handicap golfer – akin to you and me – striving relentlessly to elevate their game. Picture the scenes marked by sheer resolve interwoven with sporadic bursts of frustration, each shot dissected, scrutinized, and often met with a hearty dose of disappointment. This, indeed, is the saga of our golfing expedition, a struggle waged with an unyielding spirit, even as we find ourselves meandering through the rough and seeking enlightenment within the depths of sand traps.

Yet, within these trials lies a guiding light of potential. As we leaf through the pages of "Birdies, Bogeys, and Belly Laughs," a compilation meticulously curated for the devoted golfer, a glimmer of hope materializes. This tome is more than a mere anthology of narratives; it is a refuge for the exasperated golfer, a companion empathetic to the joys and sorrows that accompany our pursuit of improvement.

Within these pages, we share stories that resonate deeply with the heart of our golfing predicaments. Anecdotes of misadventures on the course that evoke smiles as we recognize the universality of our occasional wayward shots and confounding decision-making. We delve into the subtleties of golf course etiquette, where a misstep begets laughter, camaraderie, and a mutual comprehension of the unwritten rules governing the game.

Introduction

Yet, "Birdies, Bogeys, and Belly Laughs" transcends commiseration and tales of woe. It proffers something more—a glimpse into the potential joys awaiting us on this meandering journey. It beckons us to envision the flawless swing, the euphoric resonance of the ball meeting the club's sweet spot, and the elation accompanying a putt confidently sunk. Through clever anecdotes and insightful quotes, we catch a glimpse of a future where our golf game is not merely a pursuit of improvement but a source of unbridled pleasure and personal triumph.

As the frustrated mid-handicap golfer guiding the narrative, I comprehend the peaks and valleys inherent in the pursuit of golfing excellence. I, too, have wrestled with the demons of inconsistency and grappled with the intricacies of the game. However, I have also borne witness to the transformative influence of humor and shared experiences on the fairways. It is this awareness, born from my own trials and victories, that animates the pages of "Birdies, Bogeys, and Belly Laughs."

Now, esteemed reader, I extend an invitation to accompany me on this expedition. Let the tales, the laughter, and the shared instances of vexation and triumph elevate your spirits. Together, let us navigate the challenges and tribulations of golf, secure in the knowledge that we stand united. And as you turn the final page, may you be motivated to take action, to stride onto the course with renewed zeal and a newfound sense of delight. For within these tales resides the key to unlocking the joys that await us on the course!

Max Fielder

"There's nobody more confident here than me."

BROOKS KOEPKA

CHAPTER 1: RISE AND SHINE, GOLFER STYLE

As the sun peeks over the horizon, casting its warm glow on the meticulously manicured greens, golfers all around the world awaken with excitement. But before they can embark on their golfing adventures, a whimsical dance of preparation takes place. In this chapter, aptly titled 'Rise and Shine, Golfer Style,' we delve deep into the comical rituals and mischievous antics that unfold as golfers groggily navigate their way from the comfort of their beds to the bustling atmosphere of the golf course.

From sleepily searching for golf balls in the cereal box, mistakenly mistaking it for a stash of breakfast essentials, to donning mismatched socks and questionable fashion choices in the early morning haze, the morning routine of golfers never fails to bring a smile. We'll share anecdotes of golfers engaging in a wild goose chase, searching for their elusive golf shoes, only to find them tucked away in the most unexpected corners of the house.

But the laughter doesn't stop there. As golfers hastily pack their bags with clubs, balls, and a host of other essentials, they often find themselves caught in a series of comedic misadventures. Tales of tangled club covers engaging in epic battles, golfers attempting to fit an oversized umbrella into a too-narrow compartment, and discovering strange objects (like forgotten sandwiches or a lost sock) buried deep within their golf bags will have you in stitches.

So join us on this uproarious journey as we unravel the humorous side of preparing to play golf. From the bleary-eyed moments of awakening to the inevitable fashion faux pas and the bewildering discoveries within golf bags, you'll find yourself nodding in recognition and laughing out loud at the relatable experiences we've uncovered.

Rise and Shine, Golfer Style: The crack of dawn breaks, and groggy golfers stumble out of bed, their minds already preoccupied with visions of perfect drives and sinking putts. In their sleep-addled state, they embark on their morning rituals, blissfully unaware of the hilarity that ensues. Picture a golfer desperately searching for his lost golf balls, only to find them nestled inconspicuously amidst the cereal boxes. Others, in a state of disarray, don mismatched socks—a fashion choice best described as "eccentric elegance."

And let's not forget the fashionably challenged golfers who accidentally don their trousers backward, only realizing their sartorial misstep when they attempt to slip their hands into the non-existent pockets. Oh, the amusing spectacles of the golfer's morning routine!

In the world of golf, the morning is a time of peculiar habits and endearing idiosyncrasies. It is a time when golfers, fueled by anticipation and perhaps a cup of strong coffee, engage in a series of comical rituals that set the stage for their conquest of the golf course. As the sun peeks over the horizon, casting a golden glow upon the fairways, let us delve into the whimsical world of preparing to play golf.

Golfers are known to possess an uncanny ability to misplace their golf balls in the most unexpected places. The morning routine often begins with a groggy golfer scouring the kitchen, lifting cereal boxes, and peering into coffee mugs in a desperate quest to locate their prized orbs. With a mix of relief and amusement, they discover their lost treasures nestled amongst the breakfast provisions, as if the golf balls themselves have decided to partake in the morning feast.

And then there are the socks. Ah, the notorious mismatched socks, an inadvertent fashion statement that can only be appreciated by the truly eccentric. As golfers slip their feet into their golf shoes, they often find themselves confronted with a mismatched pair that could rival the wildest patterns of any fashion runway. Stripes clash with polka dots, argyle squares dance with floral swirls, and yet, somehow, this bold sartorial choice becomes a badge of honor, a declaration of individuality that sets golfers apart from the fashionably conforming masses.

But let us not forget the unfortunate souls who, in their pre-coffee haze, manage to defy the basic principles of dressing. Their trousers, worn backward, present a rather confounding enigma. As they attempt to slide their hands into the non-existent pockets, a look of bewilderment spreads across their faces, quickly followed by a chuckle and a sheepish adjustment. Oh, the trials and tribulations of morning dress, where even the simplest of tasks can lead to a momentary lapse in sartorial acumen.

The morning routine of golfers is a tapestry of amusing moments that set the stage for the day's golfing adventures.

From the quest for misplaced golf balls to the bold fashion choices that redefine eccentricity, these comical rituals encapsulate the charm and camaraderie of the golfing world. As golfers emerge from their sleepy stupor and step onto the dew-kissed fairways, they carry with them the laughter and lightheartedness that come from embracing the delightful absurdities of the morning routine.

Battle of the Golf Bag: Ah, the eternal struggle of organizing golf clubs—a challenge that often rivals the complexity of solving a Rubik's Cube. Witness the entangled web of club covers as golfers valiantly attempt to rescue their drivers from the depths of a tangled mess. Each morning, as golfers unzip their bags, they embark on a journey akin to unraveling a mysterious puzzle, where the clink of metal against metal becomes the soundtrack of determination.

With furrowed brows and a twinkle of anticipation in their eyes, golfers embark on a quest to locate the perfect club for every shot. But within the cavernous depths of the golf bag lies a symphony of chaos waiting to be discovered. The sight of a golfer, beads of perspiration forming on their forehead, valiantly trying to squeeze an oversized umbrella into a compartment meant for delicate tees provides a comedic ballet of determination and futility. It's a dance where frustration and amusement waltz together, leaving both the golfer and onlookers in stitches.

And what curious artifacts lie dormant within the depths of the golf bag? Forgotten sandwiches, remnants of yesterday's lunch, or perhaps a lost sock seeking solace amidst the irons? The golf bag, like a secret chamber of surprises, holds a cache of unexpected treasures that add an extra layer of intrigue to the game. Golfers rummage through their bags, discovering remnants of past rounds and whimsical mementos that bear witness to their golfing adventures. It's a delightful and humorous reminder that golf is not just about the swing but also about the stories and memories woven into the fabric of the game.

In the battle of the golf bag, golfers face a dual challenge—keeping their clubs organized while uncovering the hidden gems that lurk within. It's a dance between efficiency and curiosity, where golfers strive for order amidst the chaos, only to stumble upon a forgotten token of their golfing journey. The golf bag becomes a portal to a world of unexpected surprises and jovial exasperation, reminding golfers that even amidst the quest for precision and technique, laughter and amusement can be found.

So, next time you see a golfer engaged in an elaborate tug-of-war with their golf bag, take a moment to appreciate the comedy of the moment. It is within this battle that the camaraderie of the game shines, as fellow golfers exchange knowing glances, empathizing with the struggle and sharing in the joy of the game's quirks. The battle of the golf bag is a testament to the resilience and tenacity of golfers, who tackle each round with a sense of humor and a determination to conquer the challenges that lie in their path.

The Quest for the Perfect Swing: With clubs in hand, golfers embark on an eternal quest for the elusive perfect swing—a pursuit fraught with comedic missteps and exaggerated theatrics. Prepare to be entertained as we delve into the hilarious world of golfers' relentless determination to achieve that flawless swing, often at the expense of common sense and household harmony.

Enter the living rooms of passionate golfers, where the boundaries between golfing and domestic life blur into a whimsical dance. Behold the sight of golfers swinging at imaginary balls, their eyes fixed on an invisible target as they twirl and pivot, oblivious to the delicate china ornaments and treasured family heirlooms perilously close to their swinging arcs. Witness the heart-stopping moments when a sudden thud sends a collective gasp through the room, only to be followed by relieved laughter as a narrowly avoided disaster is met with a sigh of relief and a sheepish grin.

Witness the elaborate routines, with arms swirling like the blades of a windmill and legs kicking up in an almost acrobatic display. It is a sight that elicits both admiration and laughter, as golfers twist and turn, embracing the absurdity of their warm-up rituals with a smile.

Indeed, the quest for the perfect swing is a journey paved with laughter. Golfers, driven by an unwavering passion, immerse themselves in the pursuit of that elusive swing, fully aware of the countless mishaps and humorous incidents that come along the way. The pursuit of perfection often leads to unexpected outcomes—a swing that sends the ball hurtling in an unintended direction or a grand flourish that results in an unfortunate loss of balance and a tumble onto the turf.

Yet, amidst the laughter, there is an underlying truth. The quest for the perfect swing is not just about achieving technical precision; it is about embracing the joy, the camaraderie, and the sheer fun that golf brings. It is about relishing the shared moments of laughter, the bonds forged on the fairways, and the stories that weave their way into the fabric of the game.

So, join us as we navigate the comical twists and turns of the quest for the perfect swing. Delight in the imaginative scenarios, the exaggerated theatrics, and the light-hearted camaraderie that emerge as golfers embark on this timeless journey. From the living rooms to the practice ranges, the pursuit of the perfect swing is a testament to the enduring spirit of the game—and a reminder that sometimes, the greatest pleasure lies not in achieving perfection, but in the laughter-filled pursuit itself.

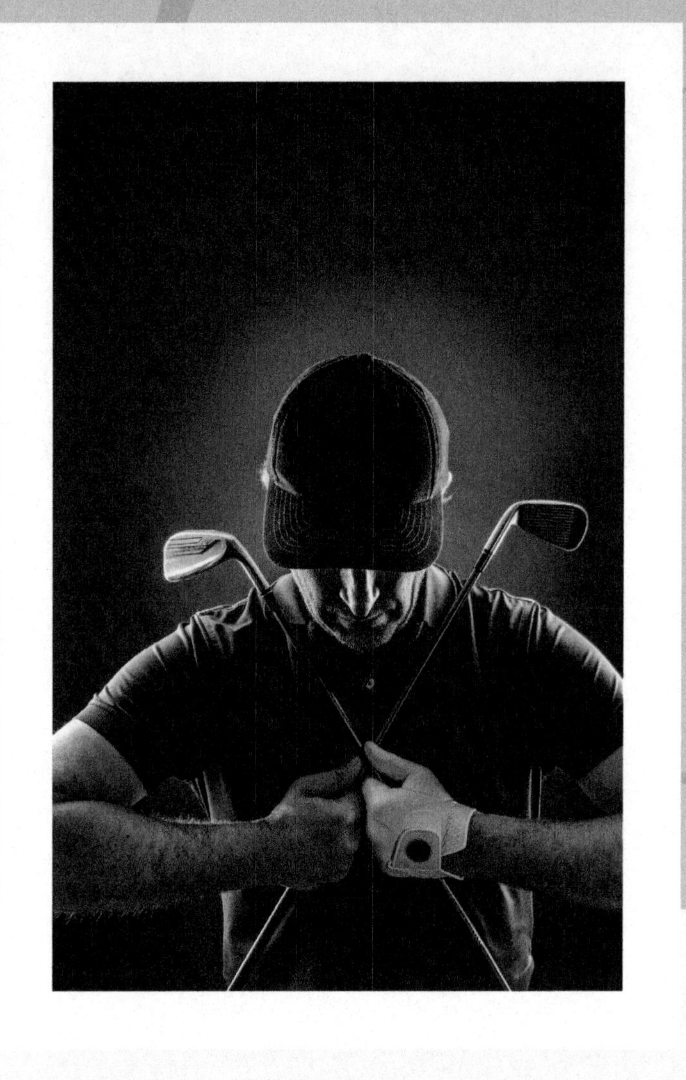

"I know I am getting better at golf because I am hitting fewer spectators."

GERALD R. FORD

CHAPTER 2: THE FUNNIEST EXCUSES EVER UTTERED AFTER A SHANKED SHOT

"Must have been a magnetic anomaly. Those power lines threw my clubhead right off!"

"Just trying a new 'slicing backspin' technique. Looks like it needs a few tweaks."

"The wind must have been changing directions faster than my partner changes their mind about dinner plans."

"Obviously, my club mistook that divot for a gopher and tried to swat it. Brave club, but foolish."

"My swing's so smooth, it hypnotized the ball mid-air. Now it's just chillin' in the rough, livin' its best life."

"This club's haunted. Last owner was a grumpy groundskeeper, and his grudge against shanked shots lives on."

"Just testing out my new 'reverse ricochet' shot. Still a work in progress, but the neighbors got a heck of a show."

"I think I accidentally sneezed during my backswing. Turns out, that's not the 'explosive power' they meant."

"That wasn't a shank, it was a strategically placed 'grounder' to avoid hitting the millionaire in the next fairway. You're welcome!"

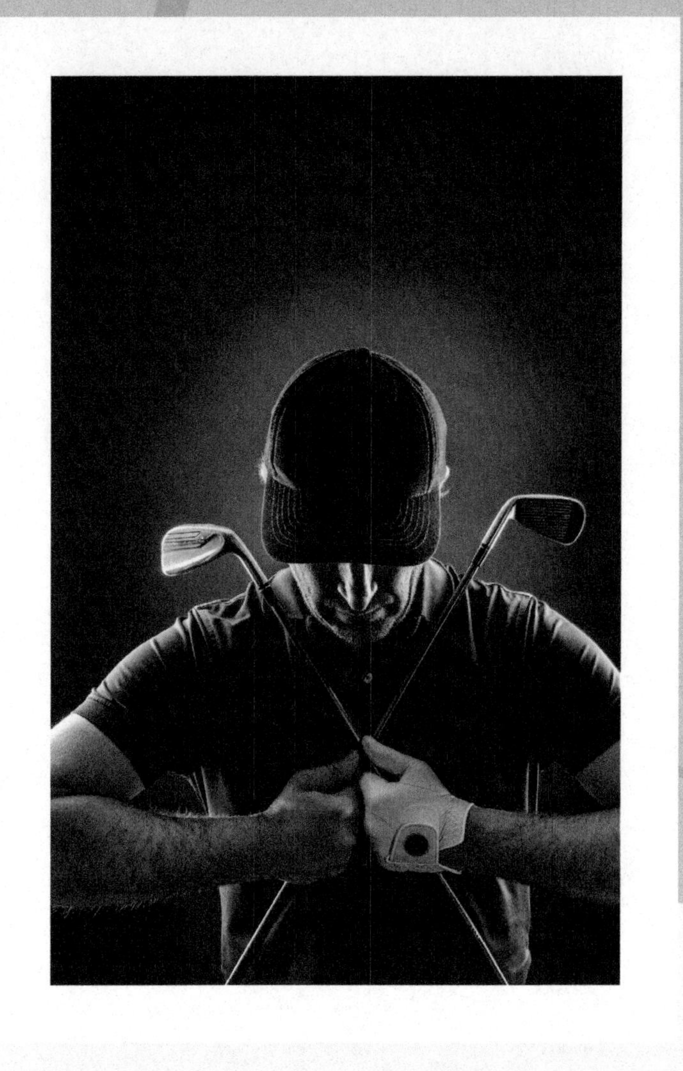

"They say golf is like life, but don't believe them. Golf is more complicated than that."

GARDNER DICKINSON

CHAPTER 3: PRACTICE AREAS: A PLAYGROUND OF PRECISION AND PECULIARITIES

The practice areas of a golf course are not merely patches of grass designated for warming up before a round. They are vibrant spaces where golfers immerse themselves in the art of improvement, embracing a myriad of peculiarities that make this realm truly unique. In this chapter, we delve into the captivating world, revealing the comical rituals and endearing idiosyncrasies that unfold as golfers converge to fine-tune their skills and master their swings. Welcome to the playground of precision and entertainment - the practice areas.

A Prelude to the Game: As golfers step onto the practice areas, a sense of anticipation fills the air, igniting the embers of excitement that lie dormant within them. The practice tee, like an artist's canvas, transforms into a captivating masterpiece, with neatly arranged rows of golfers, each akin to a musician tuning their instruments before a grand symphony. This sacred ground sets the stage for the forthcoming challenge that awaits them on the sprawling green fairways.

In the early morning light, the dew-kissed grass welcomes each golfer's footsteps, creating a harmonious rhythm that resonates with the promise of a new day filled with possibilities. As the sun slowly ascends, casting its golden hue across the landscape, a serene aura envelops the practice area, evoking a profound connection between man and nature.

Each golfer approaches this hallowed ground with a unique purpose, their hearts aligned with the pursuit of mastering this ancient and noble game. With a reverential silence, they begin their ritualistic preparations, immersing themselves in the moment, seeking a spiritual connection with the club, the ball, and the very essence of golf.

The veteran players, with weathered hands and knowing smiles, draw upon their reservoirs of experience to craft their practice routine. They understand that these moments of solitude, spent in communion with the game, are the foundation upon which greatness is built. The novices, on the other hand, wear expressions of both excitement and apprehension, aware that every swing is a step towards unraveling the enigmatic mysteries of golf.

Like a conductor leading an orchestra, the seasoned golfers guide their bodies through well-rehearsed motions, a symphony of fluidity and grace. Each swing is deliberate, every movement a carefully orchestrated dance between mind and muscle. They feel the rhythm of the game, an intangible heartbeat that courses through the fairways and resonates within their souls.
Yet, amidst the grace and fluidity, there is also room for experimentation. The practice tee becomes a laboratory for innovation, a place where golfers can push the boundaries of their abilities and explore the uncharted realms of their potential. It is a sanctuary where creativity thrives, where risk and reward coexist in perfect balance.

The air is filled with the melodious symphony of club meeting ball, a harmonious fusion of sound that encapsulates the essence of the sport. Each strike becomes a brushstroke on the canvas of the practice tee, forming an intricate tapestry of golfing tales waiting to be written on the courses ahead.

As the sun climbs higher, the practice tee transforms into a vibrant tapestry of colors, with golf balls soaring through the air like ethereal butterflies. Laughter and camaraderie emerge from the silence, as golfers exchange stories, advice, and encouragement. The fellowship of the golfing community strengthens, binding them together through their shared love for this timeless sport.

Time seems to dance to a different tempo in this realm, where worries dissipate, and the outside world fades away. The practice tee becomes a sanctuary of tranquility, where golfers can escape the cacophony of modern life and immerse themselves in the simplicity and purity of the game.

As the shadows grow longer, the practice session draws to a close, but the spirits of the golfers remain alight with the flame of passion that burns within them. They know that this prelude to the game is merely a prologue to the grand tale that awaits them on the fairways and greens.

With hearts brimming with anticipation and minds steeled with determination, the golfers step forth from the practice tee, ready to embrace the challenge ahead. They carry with them the lessons learned, the moments cherished, and the camaraderie forged during this sacred prelude. For in the realm of golf, every chapter begins with a prelude – a symphony of practice, a dance of determination, and a celebration of the timeless connection between man, nature, and the spirit of the game.

.

The Art of Mimicry: One cannot help but notice the amusing spectacle of golfers gathered on the practice area, each one attempting to emulate the iconic poses and swings of golfing legends with exaggerated flair. It's a sight that brings a smile to the faces of both players and onlookers alike. This unique aspect of the game, known as the Art of Mimicry, not only pays homage to golfing idols but also fosters a sense of lighthearted camaraderie among players.

As the sun rises on the pristine greens, golfers of all levels and backgrounds assemble at the practice area, preparing for a day of play. Among them are seasoned golfers, aspiring amateurs, and curious beginners, all drawn together by their shared passion for the sport. The Art of Mimicry serves as a unifying force, breaking down barriers and creating a sense of belonging in the golfing community. When a golfer playfully mimics the graceful backswing of a Fred Couples or attempts the charismatic follow-through of an Arnold Palmer, they not only pay tribute to these legends but also form a bond with fellow enthusiasts who recognize and appreciate the gestures.

The Art of Mimicry is a testament to the enduring legacy of golfing legends. Through the ages, legendary players have left an indelible mark on the game, inspiring generations of golfers with their unique styles and achievements. By emulating these greats, golfers not only celebrate their prowess but also keep their memories alive on the fairways. As each swing mirrors a legendary player's iconic move, their spirit seems to echo through time, resonating with every golfer paying tribute.

While the Art of Mimicry celebrates golfing legends, it also underscores the individuality of each player. No two swings are exactly alike, and that is part of the beauty of the game.

As golfers emulate the greats, they infuse their unique personalities and styles into the gestures, making them their own. In this way, the Art of Mimicry becomes a reflection of each golfer's journey and growth, highlighting the personal touch they bring to the sport.

Golf can be an intense and challenging sport, testing a player's skills, patience, and mental fortitude. The Art of Mimicry, however, introduces a delightful dose of humor and light-heartedness to the game. As players gather in the practice area, they engage in friendly banter and good-natured ribbing, lightening the atmosphere and alleviating the pressures that come with competitive play. It serves as a reminder that golf is not just about technique and scores, but also about enjoying the company of fellow golfers and having fun on the course.

Beyond the laughter and camaraderie, the Art of Mimicry also has practical benefits. When golfers imitate the moves of golfing legends, they inadvertently absorb some of the nuances and techniques that make those swings so effective. Through this playful imitation, golfers refine their own skills, discover new aspects of their game, and gain insights that can enhance their performance.

The Art of Mimicry is a delightful and endearing aspect of the game that brings together golfers in a spirit of camaraderie, reverence, and laughter. It celebrates the legacy of golfing legends while embracing the unique individuality of each player. As golfers gather on the practice area, imitating the graceful swings of iconic players, they forge bonds that transcend skill levels and backgrounds.

The Sound Barrier Shatterers: In every practice area, there exists a special breed of golfer known as "The Sound Barrier Shatterers." These individuals, driven by an insatiable blend of enthusiasm and adrenaline, unleash thunderous swings that reverberate through the air like echoing canyons.

It is as if their golf clubs produce sonic booms with each fierce strike of the ball. While their style may not always guarantee pinpoint accuracy, these golfers inject an undeniable element of exhilaration and raw power into the surroundings. The Sound Barrier Shatterers embody the essence of passion for the game. Their eyes light up at the mere thought of a golf club in their hands, and their hearts race with excitement as they approach the practice area.

While the Sound Barrier Shatterers exude an awe-inspiring display of force, it is essential to explore the delicate balance between power and control in golf. The potential trade-offs between power and accuracy, acknowledging that controlled aggression is often the key to achieving the desired results. By understanding this dynamic, golfers can learn to harness their inner strength while maintaining precision and consistency in their swings.

The Sound Barrier Shatterers may not always hit the fairway or green with every mighty swing, but their fearless approach teaches us an invaluable lesson in embracing imperfections. They encourage golfers to shed the fear of failure and instead focus on the growth that comes from taking risks and pushing beyond their comfort zones. Learning to accept the occasional wayward shot as part of the journey towards improvement can lead to breakthroughs in both physical and mental aspects of the game.

Beyond the practical implications, the Sound Barrier Shatterers add a spectacle to the golf course practice areas. The thunderous roars of their swings become a rallying cry, drawing fellow golfers and spectators alike to witness their awe-inspiring displays of power. This celebrates the allure of golf as both a competitive sport and a source of entertainment, acknowledging the unique allure that these individuals bring to the game.

The world of professional golf boasts legendary players who have mastered the art of powerful yet precise swings. The techniques and wisdom of golfing greats known for their ability to unleash remarkable power while maintaining control and accuracy. By studying the techniques employed by these masters, aspiring golfers can develop their own blend of power and finesse, bringing them closer to the level of the golfing elites.

The Art of Reading Greens: At the core of putting mastery lies the ability to read the greens. Each putt unravels as a story, with the green surface as the canvas and the ball's journey as the narrative. Golfers take their stance, carefully studying the subtle nuances of the grass, interpreting the influence of slopes, and gauging the impact of weather conditions. This dance of analysis and intuition becomes an essential skill as players assess the direction and speed required to guide the ball into the awaiting cup.

The practice putting green provides a haven for golfers to hone their putting strokes, refining the mechanics of their swing until it becomes a natural extension of their intent. The gentle pendulum-like motion of the putter takes center stage as players seek to strike the ball with precision and control. This seemingly simple movement becomes an intricate symphony of muscles working in harmony, where consistency is paramount.

Beyond the mechanics, putting is a psychological journey. In the putter's haven, golfers confront their inner battles—the demons of doubt and the triumphs of self-belief. This sacred space becomes a testing ground for mental fortitude, as players learn to silence distractions, embrace pressure, and trust their instincts. The ability to stay present in the moment and execute with composure can be the deciding factor between triumph and defeat.

In the putter's haven, perfection is the elusive prize that drives golfers to return time and again. As players sink putt after putt, the pursuit of that flawless stroke becomes an obsession—a never-ending quest to chase an ideal that remains tantalizingly just out of reach. But in this pursuit, golfers discover the true essence of the sport—where mastery is a journey, not a destination.

Beyond the technicalities and mental challenges, the practice putting green serves as a refuge from the outside world. As the sun sets and the shadows lengthen, golfers find solace in this serene corner of the golf course. Here, they can relish the camaraderie of fellow golfers sharing stories, laughter, and insights, creating bonds that endure beyond the game.

Leaving the putter's haven, golfers carry with them newfound wisdom and an insatiable appetite to keep improving. Whether facing the challenges of a championship or savoring the tranquility of a casual round, the lessons learned in this sacred space stay close to heart. The pursuit of the perfect putt is a lifelong journey, and the putter's haven becomes an enduring symbol of dedication, passion, and the unwavering spirit of the golfer.

The putter's haven embodies the essence of golf—the pursuit of excellence and the celebration of the journey. This secluded corner of the practice green holds the keys to unlocking the art of putting, elevating the golfer's game to new heights. Step into this hallowed sanctuary, and you will emerge not only as a better putter but also as a golfer with a profound appreciation for the intricate dance between the golfer, the ball, and the greens—the symphony that encapsulates the soul of golf.

The Errant Ball Adventure: As golfers immerse themselves in the tranquil ambiance of golf course practice areas, they occasionally bear witness to a phenomenon that adds an element of unpredictability and amusement to their routines - the Errant Ball Adventure. Despite the best intentions and laser-focused concentration, golf balls have a mischievous tendency to stray from their intended path, leading them on daring escapades that leave both players and onlookers in awe.

Picture this: a golfer stands on the practice tee, perfectly poised to strike the ball with precision. As the clubhead meets the ball, a resounding crack echoes through the air, but instead of soaring majestically down the range, the ball decides to take a different trajectory. It stealthily rolls across the dew-kissed grass, making its way towards a neighboring golfer's practice area. A collective gasp emanates from the spectators, followed by chuckles of amusement as the ball continues its adventure.

Observing the ball encroach upon someone else's practice space, golfers can't help but exchange knowing glances. It's a moment of camaraderie as they realize that errant shots can happen to anyone.

The neighboring golfer, startled by the unexpected visitor, might offer a light-hearted grin before casually returning the stray ball, adding a touch of goodwill to the golfing community.

The Unforeseen Rebound: Sometimes, the Errant Ball Adventure takes an unexpected turn when a stray shot finds an unconventional path to return to its rightful place. A poorly executed swing might result in the ball caroming off an obstacle - a tree, a signpost, or even a fellow golfer's golf bag - only to sail gracefully back towards its originator. It's a moment of poetic justice, where the laws of physics seem to bend playfully, providing a valuable lesson in the art of humility.

These errant ball excursions add a touch of excitement to the otherwise routine practice sessions. They remind golfers that perfection is an elusive pursuit and that the unpredictable nature of the game is what makes it so endearing. Each adventurous ball serves as a gentle reminder to take the sport with a grain of humor and enjoy the journey, regardless of its unforeseen twists and turns.

The Errant Ball Adventure is an integral part of the golfing experience on practice grounds. These daring escapades entertain, bond golfers together, and teach valuable lessons about resilience and good sportsmanship.

Embracing the comical nature of errant shots, golfers find solace in the shared experiences, forging lasting memories on their golfing journey. So, the next time your ball takes an unexpected detour, embrace the adventure, smile, and remember that in the game of golf, it's not just the destination but the journey that truly counts.

The Perfect Swings and the Imperfect Ones: Embracing the Journey in Golf Course Practice Areas. The practice areas of a golf course provide a sacred ground for golfers to refine their skills, to challenge their limits, and to embrace the profound duality of the game. Within these hallowed spaces, golfers of all levels, from beginners to seasoned professionals, embark on a journey of self-discovery and improvement.

We delve into the experiences and lessons found amidst the perfect swings and the imperfect ones, highlighting the unique beauty that emerges from the blend of triumph and trial on the practice grounds.

The Quest for Perfection: As golfers step onto the practice tee, they are fueled by a desire for perfection. With visions of silky-smooth swings and soaring shots, they diligently work to fine-tune their techniques. The pursuit of the elusive "perfect swing" becomes an obsession, as they seek to mirror the greats of the game. Through dedication and focus, some may achieve moments of greatness, basking in the satisfaction of executing a flawless shot. However, they soon discover that perfection is fleeting, and even the most skilled golfers encounter the occasional misstep.

The Inner Golf Demons: Within the confines of the practice areas, golfers grapple with their inner golf demons. Doubt, frustration, and impatience lurk in the shadows, ready to sabotage their efforts. The imperfect swings become the battleground for conquering these mental adversaries. It is in these moments of struggle that the true character of a golfer is forged. Learning to embrace the challenges and setbacks becomes essential for growth, as they begin to understand that progress often emerges from navigating through the rough patches.

Embracing Imperfection: As golfers come to terms with the inevitability of imperfect swings, they discover the beauty of imperfection itself. The game of golf is a mirror of life's imperfections and uncertainties. Through the prism of golf, they learn to find acceptance and grace in the face of adversity. Embracing imperfection fosters humility, resilience, and a deeper appreciation for the journey rather than the destination. The imperfect swings become the stepping stones to progress, as golfers learn from their mistakes and evolve as players and individuals.

Lessons from the Masters: Insights and anecdotes from legendary golfers illuminate the path of self-discovery on the practice areas. From the tales of Ben Hogan's relentless pursuit of perfection to Jack Nicklaus's ability to rebound from setbacks, the experiences of these golfing icons serve as beacons of inspiration. Their stories demonstrate that even the greatest players faced moments of imperfection and self-doubt, but it was their unwavering determination and resilience that set them apart.

The Power of Mindfulness: Amidst the quest for perfection, the practice areas offer golfers an opportunity to cultivate mindfulness. Being present in each swing, embracing the nuances of the moment, and letting go of past mistakes are vital components of mindful practice. The importance of a focused and present mind during practice sessions is crucial in helping golfers harness the power of the mind-body connection.

In the practice areas of a golf course, the interplay of perfect swings and imperfect ones creates a tapestry of experiences that enriches the golfer's journey. Here, golfers come to understand that perfection is not the ultimate goal but rather a fleeting and elusive companion on the path to improvement.

The practice areas become a sanctuary of growth, where golfers learn to embrace imperfection, conquer their inner golf demons, and cultivate mindfulness. In the ebb and flow of triumph and trial, the beauty of golf reveals itself, as it humbles and inspires in equal measure, leaving golfers with a profound appreciation for the sport's timeless wisdom.

In conclusion, the practice areas of a golf course encompass a fascinating tapestry of human nature, ranging from precision-driven discipline to comical entertainment. As golfers converge to hone their skills, they become part of a grand tradition that celebrates both the pursuit of excellence and the joy of shared experiences. Whether you're a seasoned player seeking to refine your game or a beginner finding your footing, the practice areas offer a haven where the spirit of golf comes alive in all its endearing peculiarities. So, step onto the hallowed grounds of the practice areas, and embrace the journey of improvement and discovery what lies ahead.

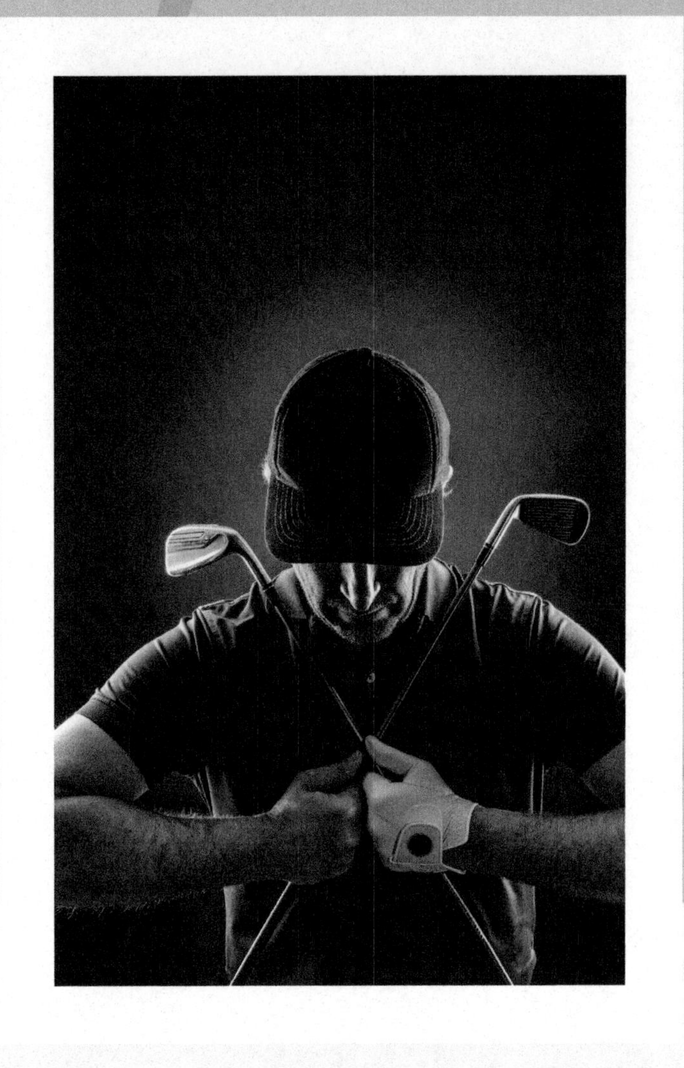

"If you think it's hard to meet new people, try picking up the wrong golf ball."

JACK LEMMON

CHAPTER 4: THE FUNNIEST EXCUSES EVER UTTERED AFTER A MISSED PUTT

"The gravitational pull of that other golfer's cart must have been messing with the green's curvature."

"Those blades of grass were clearly conspiring against me. They're like tiny, green mafia enforcers."

"I swear, the hole moved! It was definitely closer a minute ago."

"My putter must be lactose intolerant, because it just rejected that putt like spoiled milk."

"The wind held its breath just as I swung. Clearly, it's jealous of my putting prowess."

"That putt was so good, it transcended the physical realm and entered a state of pure golfing nirvana. You just wouldn't understand."

"My shoelace knew I needed some extra practice, so it strategically tripped me up just before the putt."

"I'm not sure what's worse: missing this putt or the existential dread it's causing me about the meaning of life and the universe."

"Fine, you win, putt. But just wait until next time. I'll be back, and I'll be better. And I'll probably still miss, but hey, at least I can laugh at myself, right?"

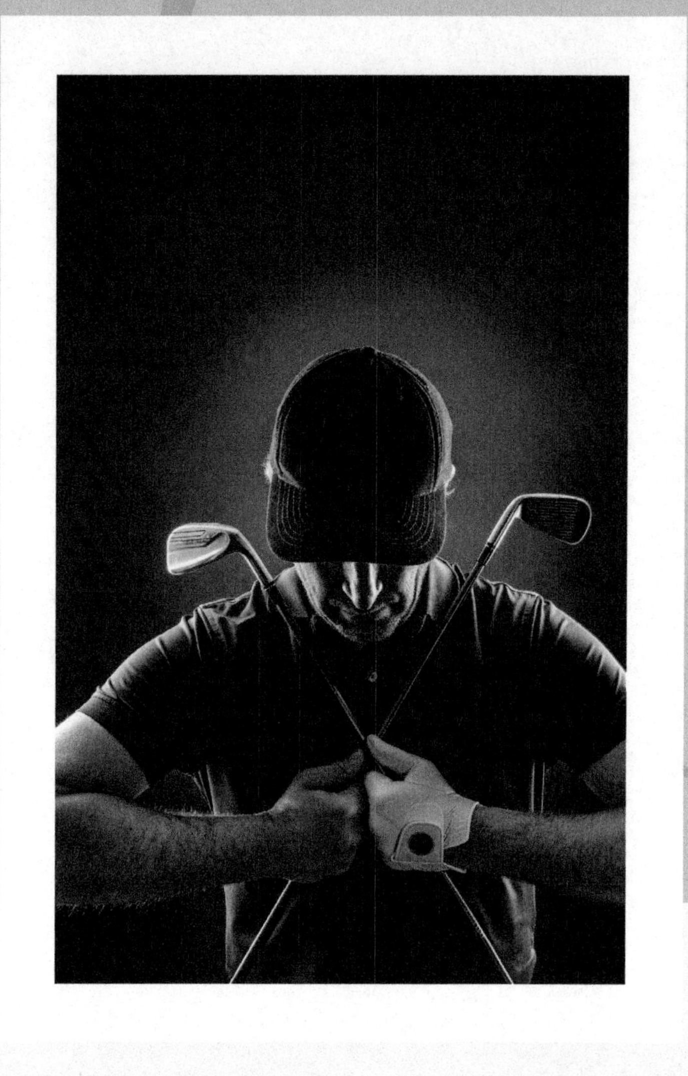

"The only thing a golfer needs is more daylight."

BEN HOGAN

CHAPTER 5: THE COMEDY OF GOLF COURSE ETIQUETTE

In the world of golf, where rules and decorum reign supreme, there exists a subtle dance of etiquette that adds an extra layer of charm to the game. Amidst the hushed whispers and meticulous attention to golfing propriety, a hidden realm of hilarity awaits, ready to unveil the comedic tapestry woven by well-intentioned golfers. Welcome to a chapter that peels back the layers of golf course etiquette, revealing the side-splitting encounters, blunders, and unexpected twists that play out against the backdrop of this refined sport.

Within the confines of golfing decorum, a treasure trove of comedic moments unfolds. Picture a golfer meticulously aligning their putt, only to have a mischievous squirrel dart across the green, distracting both player and ball. Or imagine the delightful mix-up that occurs when two golfers, engrossed in a friendly conversation, inadvertently putt each other's balls, leaving them bewildered and the gallery in fits of laughter. These moments, seemingly incongruous with the seriousness of the game, inject a playful energy into the tapestry of golf course etiquette.

As we delve deeper, prepare to be entertained by the hilarious faux pas that befall golfers attempting to master the art of polite conversation. From misjudged whispers carried away by mischievous gusts of wind to accidentally sharing personal secrets with unsuspecting nearby players, the delicate dance of golf course conversations reveals unexpected comedic gems.

So, join us as we shine a light on the lighter side of golfing decorum, where laughter intertwines with tradition and moments of mirth become the colorful threads in the fabric of the game. Through amusing encounters, blunders, and unforeseen twists, we unravel the true essence of golf course etiquette—one that embraces laughter, camaraderie, and the understanding that even amidst the strictest rules, there is always room for laughter.

The Art of the Golf Handshake: A firm grip, eye contact, and a hearty handshake—the timeless ritual that signifies camaraderie and sportsmanship in the golfing world. It's a gesture as old as the game itself, steeped in tradition and a shared understanding of respect. Yet, even the simplest of gestures can take an unexpected turn towards hilarity, turning a moment of connection into a comedic masterpiece.

In this chapter, we delve into the realm of golf handshakes, exploring the humorous scenarios that arise from misjudged grips, awkwardly timed gestures, and the occasional mix-up of hands that leave bemused golfers sharing a momentary connection that defies the conventions of the traditional handshake.

Picture this: two golfers, both equally determined and eager to showcase their sportsmanship, approach each other at the end of a hard-fought match. As they extend their hands, ready to seal the game with a handshake, destiny intervenes with a humorous twist. One golfer, their mind still reeling from a missed putt, offers a handshake that's a little too firm, inadvertently turning a friendly gesture into a mild hand-crushing contest. The other golfer, caught off guard by this unexpected display of strength, attempts to maintain composure but can't help but wince in silent agony. A moment of camaraderie transformed into a comedy of handshakes.

But misjudging the strength of a handshake is just the tip of the iceberg. Timing, it seems, is everything. Imagine two golfers, engaged in a friendly banter throughout the round, approaching the 18th hole with a shared sense of camaraderie. They swing, they chip, and they putt their way to the green, all the while exchanging jokes and laughter. As the final ball drops into the hole, the golfers instinctively extend their hands for the customary handshake. However, in a moment of comedic synchrony, their timing is slightly off. One extends their hand a fraction of a second too early, while the other extends theirs a fraction of a second too late. What ensues is a comical dance of hands, a momentary fumbling that leads to laughter and a shared understanding that sometimes, even the simplest of gestures can require impeccable timing.

Then there are those instances where a mix-up of hands turns a conventional handshake into a moment of delightful confusion. Two golfers, caught up in the excitement of a friendly match, approach each other with outstretched hands. But in an unforeseen twist of fate, their hands meet in a misaligned grip, defying the expected pattern. Left hands intertwine with right hands, fingers entangled in a dance. Bemused by this accidental connection, the golfers share a brief moment of laughter, their hands releasing and finding their proper places, all while breaking the norms of the traditional handshake.

These are just a few examples of the countless hilarious scenarios that unfold within the realm of golf handshakes. In the world of golf, where tradition meets the unpredictable nature of human interaction, even the most straightforward of gestures can become a canvas for comedic brilliance. It is in these moments, where laughter transcends the rules of etiquette, that the true spirit of the game shines brightest.

The Synchronized Symphony of Whispered Conversations: Golf courses are known for their serene ambiance, where whispers carry on the wind and polite conversations meander through the fairways. However, maintaining the delicate balance between respectful hush and unintentional comedy can be a challenging feat. We explore the amusing side of whispered conversations, as golfers attempt to convey important messages or share lighthearted banter while battling against the mischievous gusts of wind that carry their words to unintended recipients.

Picture this: A golfer lines up for a crucial putt, surrounded by the hushed anticipation of fellow players and spectators. The tension is palpable, as every eye is fixed on the delicate dance between the golfer and the ball. Just as the golfer takes a deep breath, preparing to make that decisive stroke, a gust of wind playfully snatches their whispered exclamation, carrying it across the green to the unsuspecting golfer on the adjacent hole. The result? A momentary disruption of concentration as both golfers exchange bewildered glances and try to decipher the unexpected message that has intruded upon their golfing reverie.

Whispered conversations on the golf course can create moments of unintended hilarity. Golfers, in their earnest attempts to communicate discreetly, find their words carried on mischievous zephyrs, reaching the ears of unintended recipients. The most innocent of exchanges can be transformed into a comedy of errors, with golfers caught off guard by unexpected responses or bewildered expressions. A simple request for a yardage measurement can lead to a humorous exchange of mistaken identities, as players on neighboring fairways respond to a question they believe was directed at them, only to realize their error with a shared chuckle.

Misinterpretation of whispered conversations adds another layer of comedy to the symphony of golfers' voices. A golfer attempting to share a lighthearted joke with their playing partner may find themselves met with a puzzled expression or an unexpected burst of laughter from someone who inadvertently overhears the conversation. The resulting confusion can lead to mirthful exchanges and shared laughter as golfers attempt to unravel the mystery of miscommunication.

In the realm of golfing etiquette, whispered conversations provide an opportunity for both humor and camaraderie. Golfers, united by the shared experience of battling against the elements and the challenges of the course, find solace and amusement in the unexpected moments that arise from their whispered words. The golf course transforms into a stage for the mischievous symphony of golfers' voices, where laughter and camaraderie blend harmoniously with the pursuit of excellence.

Tee Time Etiquette: Step onto the tee box, where time and tradition converge in a dance of punctuality and camaraderie. In the realm of golf, tee times hold a sacred place, ensuring order amidst the flurry of swings and putts. But fear not, dear golfer, for within the bounds of tee time etiquette lies a tapestry of considerations, where punctuality intertwines with flexibility, and the rhythm of play takes center stage. Let us embark on a lighthearted journey through the guidelines of tee time management, where laughter and respect for the pace of play are paramount.

A golfer's journey begins with a scheduled tee time, a meeting point where players converge to embark on their golfing odyssey. But in this orchestration of tee times, punctuality reigns supreme. Picture this: golfers in various stages of readiness, some adorned in mismatched socks and others balancing precariously on one leg as they wrestle with their shoelaces. The dance of punctuality unfolds as golfers strive to arrive promptly, their alarm clocks echoing through the sleepy dawn, and their enthusiasm propelling them forward.

However, within this symphony of timeliness, comedic moments abound. We witness golfers frantically searching for their misplaced car keys, only to discover them hidden in the depths of their golf bags, amidst a sea of tees and forgotten snacks.

And there are those who, in their eagerness to be on time, inadvertently arrive at the wrong course, left to navigate a serendipitous journey to the correct fairway. These tales remind us that the pursuit of punctuality may occasionally veer off course, leading to laughter-filled detours along the golfing path.

Golf, with its unpredictable nature, demands a delicate balance between structure and flexibility. While tee times provide a framework for the day's play, unexpected circumstances often weave themselves into the tapestry of the game. The golfer who gracefully adjusts their plans, embracing the twists and turns with a smile, embodies the true spirit of flexibility. Imagine a group of golfers awaiting their turn on the tee, when a sudden rain shower descends upon them, turning the fairways into shimmering streams. In this moment, flexibility reigns supreme as golfers take cover beneath umbrellas, sharing tales of past golfing misadventures with a twinkle in their eyes. And then, when the clouds part and the sun's rays grace the greens once more, they resume their play with renewed vigor, a testament to the resiliency of the golfing spirit.

Golf, with its sprawling fairways and meandering paths, is a game that embraces a harmonious flow. The pace of play becomes a delicate balance between efficiency and leisure, where each golfer contributes to the symphony with their tempo. Picture a golfer engrossed in a moment of strategic contemplation, only to realize that they've inadvertently held up the group behind them. With a sheepish smile, they gracefully yield, allowing the melody of the game to continue unhindered. And then there are the tales of golfers whose passion for the game surpasses all notions of time, as they engage in elaborate pre-shot routines, consulting with their imaginary caddies and performing complex stretches. These moments of delightful eccentricity remind us that the pace of play is as diverse as the golfers themselves, each adding their unique rhythm to the grand composition of the game.

Course Courtesy: Step onto the hallowed grounds of the golf course, and you enter a world where etiquette and camaraderie reign supreme. Now we delve into the unspoken rules that guide golfers through their quest for the perfect swing.

Join us as we unravel the intricacies of course courtesy, where maintaining a respectful atmosphere, honoring the traditions of the game, and embodying the spirit of sportsmanship create a symphony of golfing decorum.

Order of Play: Ah, the delicate dance of determining the order in which golfers take their swings. A strategic ballet unfolds as players navigate the intricate web of who goes first, who waits, and who tees off amidst chuckles and camaraderie. The unspoken negotiations, playful banter, and occasional debates weave a tapestry of amusement. We share tales of golfers who try to politely defer their turn, only to realize they have unintentionally passed the torch to another. And let us not forget those humorous situations when golfers find themselves in a merry-go-round of confusion, taking turns teeing off and watching their balls collide mid-air in a colorful display of unintended comedy.

Silent Spectators: Golf is a sport that demands silence during critical moments, when a single whisper can shatter concentration. As golfers prepare to make their shots, an unspoken agreement envelops the course, and the spectators become silent guardians of the game. But within the stillness, a few mischievous souls cannot resist the temptation to push the boundaries of decorum. We recount tales of spectators whose phones accidentally ring at the most inopportune times, releasing a cacophony of whimsical ringtones. These instances, though momentarily disruptive, bring a twinkle to the eyes of both players and onlookers, reminding us that laughter is never far from the heart of the game.

Pace of Play: A Balancing Act of Efficiency and Enjoyment The rhythm of a golf round is a delicate balance between maintaining a steady pace and savoring the unfolding drama of each shot. We delve into the comical dance of golfers as they strive to find their rhythm amidst the ebb and flow of the game. From the amusing interludes of searching for lost balls to the ever-present dilemma of deciding who tees off first, the pace of play becomes a performance of patience and eagerness. We share tales of golfers caught in the battle between haste and leisure, resulting in both rib-tickling moments and a shared understanding that time on the course is meant to be cherished.

Respecting the Shots: A Gesture of Sportsmanship Golf is a game of honor, where respect for one another's shots and decisions is the foundation of fair play.

However, even the most well-intentioned gestures can veer into the realm of comedy. We unveil the lighthearted moments that occur when golfers demonstrate their respect in unexpected ways. From applauding a missed shot with enthusiasm to providing unsolicited advice that borders on hilarity, the game of golf becomes a tapestry of humorous displays of sportsmanship. These moments remind us that in the realm of golfing companionship, laughter is the ultimate bond that transcends scores and strokes.

Etiquette in Golf Club Facilities: The clubhouse, a haven of golfing camaraderie and mirth, beckons golfers to step into its hallowed halls. Within these esteemed walls, where the air is filled with the delightful buzz of conversation and the clinking of glasses, etiquette weaves its way through the tapestry of laughter and occasional comedic missteps. We invite you to peek behind the curtains of the clubhouse, where the rules of decorum and the unexpected twists of humor intertwine in a delightful dance.

Picture this: a scene of joviality and refined conviviality, where golfers gather to exchange tales of triumph and folly. Yet, even within the sanctuary of the clubhouse, comedic mishaps are never far away. We regale you with tales of mix-ups in member names, resulting in uproarious introductions that bring forth peals of laughter. Imagine the scene as Mr. Johnson extends his hand to greet Mr. Thompson, only to be met with a bemused expression and a sheepish admission of mistaken identity. These instances of mistaken names, while momentarily causing confusion, forge bonds of camaraderie that transcend the boundaries of formality.

And what of the delicate art of balancing a plate of delectable hors d'oeuvres while engaging in spirited golf banter? The clubhouse becomes a stage where golfers, caught in the delicate dance of maintaining composure and satisfying their appetites, find themselves in hilariously precarious situations. Picture Mrs. Smith, elegantly dressed in her golfing attire, attempting to savor a bite of finger food while recounting her latest golfing conquest. As she deftly balances her plate, the hors d'oeuvre precariously perched on a toothpick, a sudden burst of laughter causes a momentary lapse in her concentration. Alas, the tiny delicacy tumbles to the ground, evoking a chorus of chuckles from fellow golfers who can relate all too well to the perils of multitasking within the boundaries of golfing etiquette.

Within the clubhouse's walls, etiquette assumes a playful guise, allowing room for good-natured banter and unexpected moments of hilarity. The clinking of glasses resonates with the harmonious symphony of shared stories and infectious laughter. Here, golfers find solace in the knowledge that the pursuit of perfection on the course need not be devoid of joy and levity.

As we paint this vivid picture of clubhouse antics, we invite you to immerse yourself in a world where decorum and humor coexist, where the sacred rituals of golfing etiquette are tempered with lightheartedness and laughter. Each tale shared, each mishap recounted, serves as a gentle reminder that, while golf may be a sport steeped in tradition, it is also a realm of human connection and joyful camaraderie.

So, sip on your favorite libation, bask in the warm glow of friendship, and allow us to transport you to the heart of the clubhouse experience. Let the laughter echo through the corridors, the camaraderie fill your soul, and the delicate dance of etiquette and cdmedy guide your steps. Within these pages, etiquette becomes a conduit for lighthearted moments and shared experiences that will leave you with a smile on your face and a newfound appreciation for the laughter that permeates the sanctum of the clubhouse.

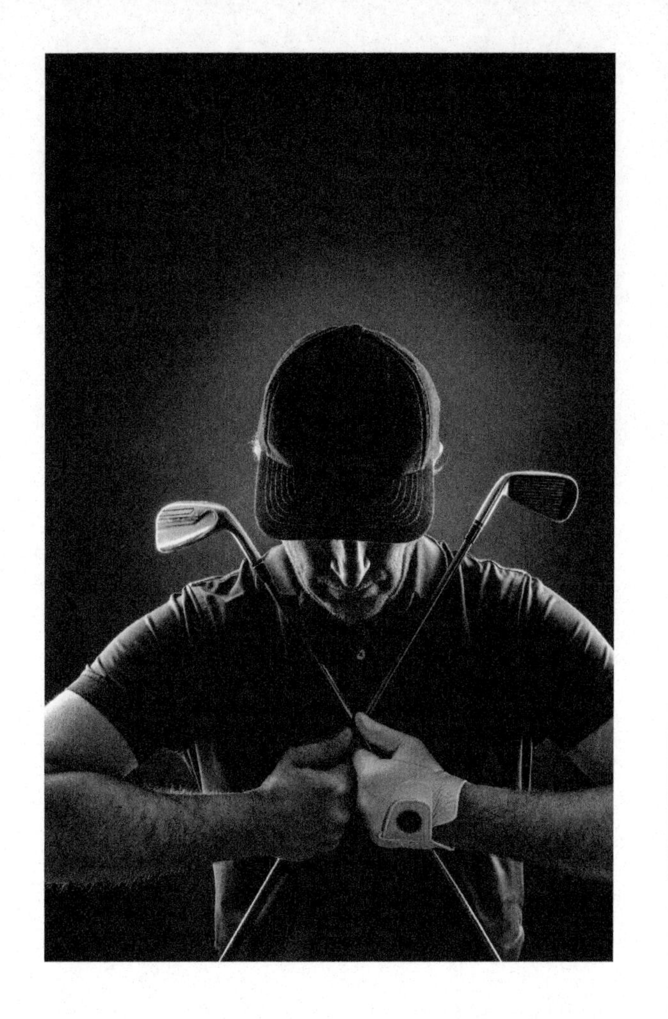

"Golf is a puzzle without an answer. I've played the game for 50 years, and I still haven't the slightest idea of how to play."

GARY PLAYER

CHAPTER 6: THE FUNNIEST EXCUSES EVER UTTERED AFTER A TEE SHOT

"Must've been a solar flare. Saw the ball launch, then poof! Disappeared into another dimension."

"My swing's like a butterfly: elegant, graceful, and completely unpredictable."

"Clearly, my driver and I are having a 'creative differences' moment. It wanted a 90-degree turn, I wanted the fairway. Looks like the driver won..."

"This club hates me. Swear it's still holding a grudge from that disastrous shank last week. Time for an exorcism... or a new driver."

"Apparently, squirrels on this course are trained in golf ball retrieval. That one just stole my shot right out of mid-air! Cheaters!"

"The wind changed allegiance halfway through my swing. Turns out, it's a fickle friend in the golfing world."

"My backswing was so pure, it launched the ball into orbit. Science experiment gone wrong, or the start of a glorious space golf program?"

"Don't worry, that was just a practice shot... for a really, really bad slice. Now let's see if I can actually hit the fairway this time..."

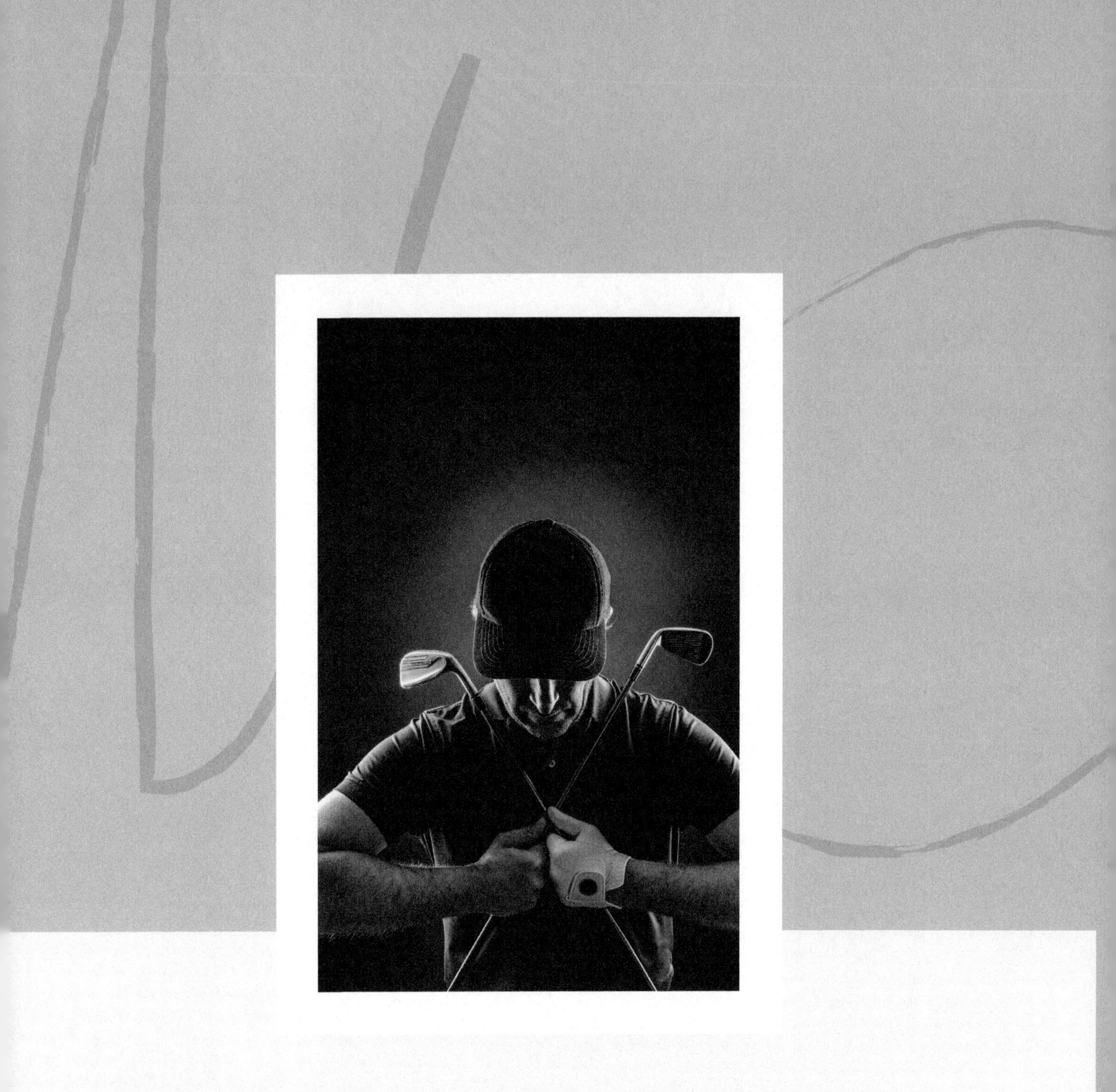

Golf is a game where you yell "Fore", shoot six and write down five

NAPOLEAN HILL

CHAPTER 7: THE QUIRKS AND CHARACTERS OF GOLF

The Unforgettable Golf Course Characters: Enter the realm of the golf course, where the tapestry of characters unfolds with vibrant hues and infectious laughter. Within the carefully manicured fairways and alongside the rolling greens, a colorful cast of personalities emerges, infusing the game with an extra dose of humor and unforgettable charm. In this chapter we invite you to meet these delightful and eccentric characters who transform each round of golf into a symphony of mirth and camaraderie.

First, we encounter the loquacious starter, a charismatic maestro of the tee box who greets golfers with a wink and a never-ending repertoire of jokes. Whether it's a groan-inducing pun or a witty one-liner, their infectious laughter sets the tone for a round filled with lightheartedness. With a twinkle in their eye, they regale golfers with humorous anecdotes, transforming the first tee into a stage for laughter and banter.

As we traverse the fairways, we encounter the mischievous squirrel, a cunning thief of golf balls. This furry bandit scampers across the greens, taunting golfers with each pilfered prize. With a flick of its tail, it watches in amusement as golfers attempt to outwit its crafty maneuvers. Stories abound of golfers engaging in playful chases with this nimble thief, their laughter mingling with the rustling of leaves as they try to reclaim their stolen treasure. The squirrel becomes a mischievous accomplice, adding an unexpected twist to the game.

But the cast of characters doesn't end there. We meet the seasoned caddie, whose sage advice is peppered with witty remarks and humorous quips. As golfers navigate the hazards and challenges of the course, these experienced guides provide not only invaluable insight but also a well-timed joke or two to lighten the mood. They become confidants, keeping golfers entertained with their quick wit and endearing stories, forging a bond that extends beyond the greens.

Then there's the resident golf course mascot, a charismatic canine whose presence brings smiles to the faces of all who encounter them. With an exuberant wag of the tail and a mischievous glint in their eyes, they become a symbol of joy and playfulness. They chase after stray balls, playfully interrupting golfers' swings, and add an element of spontaneity to the game.

Their antics become legendary, capturing the hearts of golfers and reminding them to embrace the humorous side of the sport.

Through heartfelt anecdotes and playful reminiscences, we celebrate the unforgettable encounters with these remarkable characters who leave an indelible mark on the hearts and memories of golfers. Each interaction becomes a cherished story, shared with fellow golfers over a pint at the 19th hole, as they recount the quirks, laughter, and delightful moments shared with these extraordinary individuals.

The Legendary Golf Ball Hunters: Embark on a journey with the intrepid golf ball hunters, those brave souls who venture into the uncharted realms of rough, bushes, and water hazards in pursuit of lost treasures. In this enchanting world, we regale you with amusing stories of these relentless seekers, capturing their audacious escapades and uncanny abilities that have turned golf ball retrieval into a thrilling subculture. So, don your adventure cap and join us as we delve into the delightful realm of the legendary golf ball hunters.

Picture, if you will, a golfer with the determination of a treasure hunter and the ingenuity of an inventor. Armed with a collection of gadgets and contraptions that rival a James Bond film, these resourceful individuals embark on epic quests to retrieve their wayward shots. We share tales of golfers fashioning makeshift ball retrievers from fishing rods, umbrellas, and even extendable backscratchers, transforming the pursuit of a lost ball into a grand adventure. Through their inventive exploits, these golf ball hunters prove that no obstacle is insurmountable when it comes to reclaiming their lost treasures.
But it is not just the gadgets that define these legendary hunters; it is their unyielding spirit and their uncanny ability to spot hidden gems amidst the tangled wilderness. We present stories of golfers blessed with a sixth sense for spotting lost balls, their eyes seemingly gifted with a mystical power to penetrate the thickest rough or darkest water. These extraordinary individuals stumble upon an abundance of wayward balls as if guided by an invisible hand, leaving their fellow golfers in awe and wondering if there is indeed a secret art to this captivating pursuit.

Follow us deep into the untamed territories of nature, where the golf ball hunters navigate hazards both natural and man-made. We recount their encounters with mischievous squirrels that seem intent on collecting golf balls for their own secret hoards. We witness the daring exploits of hunters braving muddy swamps, their determination unwavering as they plunge into murky waters to retrieve their sunken treasures. These tales of adventure and the audacity of the golf ball hunters will leave you both inspired and entertained, showcasing the lengths to which they are willing to go in pursuit of a lost ball.

Indeed, the golf ball-hunting subculture is a world of mystery and wonder, where ordinary golfers transform into daring adventurers. It is a realm where the thrill of discovery and the triumph of perseverance intertwine, offering a glimpse into the human spirit's indomitable quest for conquest. With each tale, we invite you to immerse yourself in the heart-pounding excitement of the hunt, where the spoils are not gold or jewels but the simple joy of finding what was once lost. So, fellow golf enthusiasts, prepare to be captivated by the legendary golf ball hunters and their extraordinary exploits. Let their stories inspire you, and perhaps, ignite your own inner adventurer, ready to embrace the challenges and triumphs that await you on the fairways and beyond.

The Masters of Golf Excuses: In the vast tapestry of golfing folklore, there exists a sacred realm known only to the craftiest of golfers—the art of weaving ingenious excuses. For in the crucible of the golf course, where scores are tallied and egos hang in the balance, a golfer's ability to conjure creative explanations for wayward shots becomes a badge of honor. Step into this world of imaginative alibis, where blame is deflected with a wink, and responsibility is artfully dodged.

Picture this: A golfer stands upon the tee, the anticipation palpable, the crowd hushed. They swing with conviction, only to see the ball slice dramatically into the neighboring fairway. It is in this moment that the true masters of golf excuses shine. They harness the power of their storytelling prowess to craft narratives that shield their golfing reputation from the blows of an errant shot.

The elusive gopher strikes again!" they exclaim, pointing dramatically towards a small mound in the distance. Yes, dear reader, the gopher —a phantom of the greens—is a favored scapegoat among those skilled in the art of excuse-making. Blaming these elusive creatures for misaligned shots has become a time-honored tradition, a way to transform a blunder into a stroke of misfortune inflicted by the hand of fate.

But the gopher is just one brushstroke on the canvas of golfing alibis. The masters of excuses have a repertoire that spans the vast spectrum of the plausible and the outrageous. They summon the classic "sun was in my eyes" excuse, even on the cloudiest of days, invoking a celestial obstruction to absolve themselves of any perceived shortcomings. They summon gusts of wind that only they can feel, insisting that nature herself conspired against their success.

In the realm of golf excuses, creativity knows no bounds. The audacious among them will blame their caddies, attributing a poor club selection to a momentary lapse in communication. Others may feign an injury—a twinge in their back, a cramp in their swing—to divert attention from a series of disappointing shots. Each excuse is a brushstroke on the canvas of their golfing narrative, a stroke of genius that shields their pride and tickles the funny bone.

As we delve into the world of these golfing maestros, tales of their inventive storytelling will unravel before your eyes, leaving you gasping for breath amidst fits of laughter. Imagine a golfer, with a straight face, asserting that their club was bewitched by a mischievous leprechaun, leading to an unpredictable trajectory. Or picture the golfer who blames an unruly gust of wind for the mysterious disappearance of their ball, as if the very elements conspired to confound their efforts.

These golfing excuses are not merely feats of imagination; they are an integral part of the game's fabric. They add a layer of intrigue, amusement, and camaraderie among players, for in sharing these tales of ingenuity, golfers find solace in knowing that they are not alone in their quest to preserve their golfing reputation.

So, dear reader, prepare to be regaled with tales of the masters of golf excuses. From the absurd to the absurdly plausible, these stories will leave you astounded by the lengths to which golfers will go to protect their pride. And who knows, perhaps these tales will ignite a spark within you, inspiring your own repertoire of plausible deniability. Let the realm of golfing excuses unveil its secrets, and may the laughter echo across fairways and greens for generations to come.

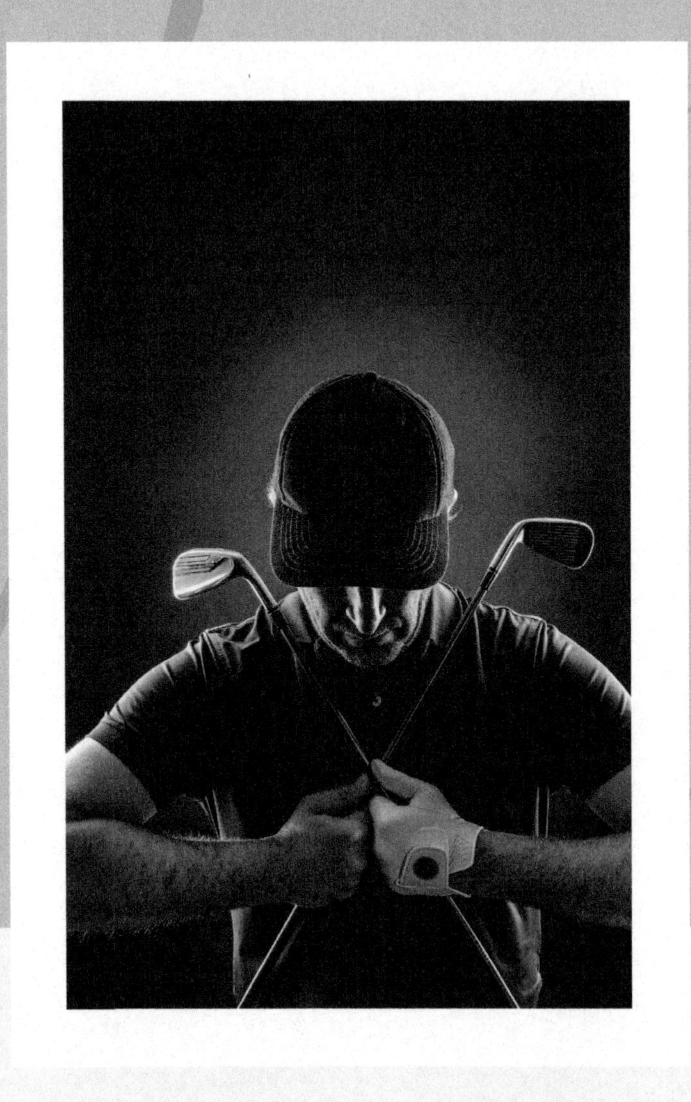

"There are three roads to ruin; women, gambling, and golf. The most pleasant is with women, the quickest is with gambling, but the surest is with golf."

ANDREW PERRY

CHAPTER 8: THE FUNNIEST EXCUSES EVER UTTERED AFTER A BUNKER SHOT

"That sand must be quicksand! My ball just swallowed itself whole."

"I think I accidentally channeled my inner mole. Oops, wrong tool for the job!"

"Must be a magnetic anomaly in this bunker. My club kept getting pulled off course."

"The wind? What wind? There's no wind... except for that hurricane suddenly swirling around my head."

"Clearly, this bunker is haunted by the ghost of a grumpy sandcastle architect. He's not a fan of my divot-making skills."

"I swear, that bunker was designed by a sadistic chipmunk. Those ridges are like tiny, taunting mountains."

"My putting prowess may be legendary, but apparently, my bunker game needs a few therapy sessions."

"Okay, fine, I admit it. I panicked. Saw the sand and my brain just went 'nope!' and sent the ball into orbit."

"I think I channeled my inner beach ball instead of a golf ball. That explains the unpredictable bounce and the surprised look on the sunbather's face."

"This bunker is clearly a portal to another dimension. My ball just vanished like a magician's disappearing act. Maybe they have better sand there?"

"If you get caught on the course during a storm and are afraid of lightning, then hold up your one-iron; even god cannot hit a one-iron."

LEE TREVINO

CHAPTER 9: ON THE GREEN: PUTTING PERILS

We invite you to embark on a laughter-filled journey through the world of putting, where the gentle tap of the ball can lead to both triumph and tribulation. In this delightful chapter, we delve into the amusing aspects of putting and uncover the hilarious challenges that golfers encounter on the green, all while sharing a collection of tales that will leave you in stitches.

Prepare to join us as we explore the perplexing physics of the perfect putt, where the subtle undulations of the green can lead even the most seasoned golfer astray. Discover the tales of golfers who find themselves caught in the treacherous web of misaligned putts, where the ball seems to have a mind of its own, veering off course and leaving the golfer bewildered and bemused.

But it's not just the whims of the green that pose challenges. We delve into the mischievous hazards that can turn a seemingly simple putt into a sidesplitting spectacle, the putting green becomes a stage for hilarity and unexpected surprises. We present an array of anecdotes that highlight the lighter side of putting, capturing the moments where frustration meets laughter and where the pursuit of a successful putt becomes a joyful and comedic endeavor.

So join us on the green, where the air is filled with anticipation, the putters are poised, and the laughs are abundant. From novices to pros, "On the Green: Putting Perils" offers a glimpse into the uproarious world of putting, reminding us that even in the face of challenges, laughter is the best companion on the journey to mastering the art of the putt.

The Art of Reading Greens: Putting, the delicate art of coaxing a ball into its final resting place on the green, is a dance that requires equal parts precision, intuition, and a dash of magic. Yet, in the enchanting realm of reading greens, even the most seasoned golfers find themselves entangled in a web of bewilderment, where slopes deceive, speeds confound, and breaks bewitch. With a mischievous glint in our eyes, we embark on a journey through the comical tales that unfold when golfers attempt to decipher the secrets hidden within the emerald tapestry of the putting surface.

Picture this: a golfer, club in hand, standing before a seemingly innocuous green. Confidence radiates from their every pore as they meticulously assess the terrain. But little do they know that the green holds secrets—secrets that will test their resolve and unleash a wave of laughter. We chuckle as golfers misjudge slopes, their carefully calculated paths thwarted by gravity's mischievous whims. Like a feline chasing a laser pointer, they watch in disbelief as their ball veers off course, defying logic and leaving them with a befuddled expression that borders on the absurd.

Ah, the speed of the greens—an ever-elusive variable that challenges even the most attuned senses. We witness golfers unleashing a delicate touch, convinced they have unraveled the mystery of the perfect pace, only to watch in amusement as their ball races past the hole like a runaway hare. The greens, it seems, possess a mischievous spirit, toying with golfers' expectations and transforming their confident strides into comedic sprints to catch up with their rogue balls.

But the breaks—the enigmatic twists and turns—truly ignite the laughter on the greens. Golfers gaze intently, envisioning a smooth path, only to have their hopes dashed as their ball takes an unforeseen detour, careening off course like a rebellious spirit breaking free from its shackles. We giggle as they scratch their heads, contemplating the mysteries of physics and pondering how a straightforward putt could morph into a perplexing puzzle.

In the world of reading greens, there are no masters, only humble apprentices attempting to decipher the intricate code etched upon the grass. The greens, it seems, possess a mischievous sense of humor, inviting golfers to dance with uncertainty, teaching them humility with each missed opportunity, and offering the occasional glimpse of triumph that keeps them coming back for more.

And so, as we immerse ourselves in the tales of misjudged slopes, lightning-fast greens, and tantalizing breaks, we find solace in the shared laughter that echoes across the golf course. For in these moments of bewilderment and joy, we discover that the art of reading greens is not merely a quest for perfection but a dance that embraces the delightful imperfections of the game.

The Adventures of the Wayward Putter: "The Adventures of the Wayward Putter" takes us deep into the realm of golfing peculiarities, where even the most reliable of golf clubs—the putter—reveals its mischievous side. As golfers strive to conquer the greens with finesse and precision, their trusty putters have a knack for misbehaving at the most inopportune moments, providing endless amusement and bewilderment.

Picture this: A golfer lines up a crucial putt, their focus sharp and their confidence soaring. They delicately swing their putter, only to witness an unexpected turn of events. Instead of gliding smoothly across the grass, the putter decides to take a detour. It wedges itself deep into the turf, creating a momentary spectacle that leaves both the golfer and onlookers in fits of laughter. The putter's mischievous nature reveals itself, reminding us that even the most essential tools of the trade can have a mind of their own.

But the adventures of the wayward putter do not stop there. In the realm of golfing hilarity, we encounter stories that defy the laws of physics. Imagine a golfer, poised to make the perfect stroke, only to witness their putter transform into a boomerang mid-swing. It spirals through the air with a mischievous gleam, looping back to its starting point with a perplexed golfer left empty-handed. Such whimsical acts of rebellion demonstrate that even the most steadfast of golf clubs can harbor a mischievous streak.

Yet, the tales of the wayward putter reach their zenith when these seemingly ordinary clubs take on a life of their own. Picture a golf course, bathed in the golden hues of twilight, as golfers line up their putts. Suddenly, chaos ensues as putters break free from their owners' grips, embarking on a spirited race across the green. With golfers in hot pursuit, the rogue putters zigzag through the obstacles, defying capture at every turn. This chase adds a touch of enchantment to the golfing experience, reminding us that there is always room for surprises on the fairways.

So, the next time you find yourself on the green, be prepared for the unexpected. Keep an eye on your trusty putter, for it may have a mischievous agenda of its own.

Embrace the adventures that unfold, whether it's witnessing your putter burrow itself into the turf, witnessing its boomerang-like tendencies, or finding yourself engaged in a spirited chase across the green. Embrace the enchantment and let the tales of the wayward putter become part of your own golfing lore.

Putting Games Gone Awry: Within the world of golf, where camaraderie and friendly competition intertwine, there exists a realm of putting games that can transform the serene greens into a laughter-filled battlefield. We invite you to witness the uproarious adventures that unfold when golfers gather to engage in putting games that push their skills, test their nerves, and challenge their ability to keep a straight face.

Amidst the rolling hills and manicured greens, a whole new dimension of merriment reveals itself as friends embark in putting games and challenges. It begins innocently enough, with playful banter and friendly wagers that add a spark of excitement to the air. But as the stakes rise, so does the potential for comedic brilliance. We delve into the tales of outrageous bets that see golfers donning ridiculous outfits or attempting putting strokes blindfolded, all in the pursuit of victory and the sweet taste of triumph.

Yet, it is in the unconventional rules and quirks of putting contests that the true hilarity emerges. Imagine a game where players must putt using a frying pan instead of a putter or one where the ball ricochets off strategically placed obstacles like garden gnomes and rubber ducks. We regale you with tales of golfers attempting precision putts while perched on one leg or battling against the distractions of squirrels pilfering their golf balls mid-putt. These absurdly delightful scenarios highlight the ingenuity, creativity, and sheer audacity that golfers bring to the game.

But it's not just the gameplay that sparks laughter; it's the reactions and interactions among players that add an extra layer of amusement. Picture a golfer desperately trying to suppress a fit of giggles as their friend's putt takes an unexpected detour and loops back towards the tee box. Or witness the mischievous glances exchanged between rivals, silently communicating their shared delight in the unpredictable nature of the game. Putting games become a stage for comedic theatrics, where golfers don the roles of jesters, jokers, and master manipulators, all for the sake of a good laugh.

The Dreaded Three-Putt Syndrome: Within the hallowed realm of golf, where precision and finesse are revered, there exists a universal dread that strikes fear into the hearts of even the most seasoned players—the dreaded three-putt syndrome. It looms like a mischievous imp, ready to snatch victory from the jaws of triumph and reduce even the most composed golfer to a state of frustration. But in the realm of golfing tales, even the dreaded three-putt can become a source of laughter and amusement, as golfers find themselves entangled in a web of comedic misfortune on the green.

Picture this: a golfer steps onto the velvety putting surface, the tension palpable in the air. All eyes are on them as they line up their shot, envisioning the ball delicately rolling into the awaiting cup. The backswing commences, the putter strikes the ball with precision, and... the ball inexplicably veers off course, missing the mark by a country mile. A collective groan ripples through the gallery, punctuated by a smattering of chuckles. It's the classic tale of the unexpected, the golfing equivalent of a punchline delivered with impeccable timing.

But why stop at a single misfortune when the golfing gods have a flair for the theatrical? Let us delve into the comedic side of the dreaded three-putt syndrome and uncover the tales of golfers who have fallen victim to its whims. Picture a golfer succumbing to the pressures of the green, their hands transforming into uncooperative clumps of butter as they attempt to delicately tap the ball into the hole. The ball slips through their fingers like a greased eel, leaving them staring in disbelief as it rolls just inches away from their intended target. Cue the laughter—a symphony of mirth that echoes across the course, punctuated by sympathetic nods and knowing grins.

Ah, but the mischievous forces at play on the green are not limited to the realm of human error alone. Consider the hapless golfer, poised to make their final putt, when suddenly a wayward squirrel scampers onto the scene. With a swift movement of its tiny paws, the squirrel sends shockwaves through the golfer's concentration, disrupting their focus just as they prepare to sink the most important shot of the day. Laughter erupts, mingling with the rustling of leaves and the scurrying of tiny feet, as the golfer's attempt at a graceful putt devolves into a clumsy dance of surprise and bewilderment.

In the tapestry of golfing tales, the dreaded three-putt syndrome takes on a life of its own—a mischievous imp that prances on the greens, teasing and taunting golfers with its capricious whims. But amidst the frustration and the groans, there lies an undeniable charm, a reminder that golf is not just about perfection, but also about embracing the unexpected and finding joy in the moments of light-hearted camaraderie that emerge from the shadows of mishaps.

So, dear reader, let us revel in the hilarity of the dreaded three-putt, relishing the tales of golfers who have danced this comedic dance on the greens. From the golfer who inadvertently putts into a bunker to the one who finds their ball perilously balanced on the lip of the cup, the tales are as diverse as the individuals who grace the fairways. And through it all, let laughter be our guiding companion, turning the dreaded three-putt into a badge of honor—a reminder that in the game of golf, the journey itself is just as important as the destination.

The Hazards of the Putting Green: Step onto the putting green, where serenity and concentration intertwine in a delicate balance, and prepare to enter a world where the unexpected is par for the course. We unravel the tapestry of hazards that lurk amidst the rolling greens, adding a touch of laughter to the art of putting.

As golfers carefully line up their shots, little do they know that mischievous insects lie in wait, ready to wreak havoc on their moment of focus. Flitting around like miniature jesters, these tiny troublemakers buzz and chirp, employing their pesky tactics to distract even the most seasoned putters. Picture a golfer, eyes locked on the ball, only to be interrupted by the persistent tickle of a mischievous mosquito or the daring acrobatics of a determined dragonfly. These airborne comedians bring a touch of chaos to the putting green, turning moments of tranquility into uproarious scenes of swatting, flailing, and laughter.

But it's not just the insect kingdom that conspires against golfers' intentions. The putting green has its own mysterious brand of magic, where balls seem to take on a life of their own. Just as a perfectly aligned putt is set in motion, the invisible gusts of wind unleash their mischievous power, redirecting balls with uncanny precision.

Witness the bewildered golfer, eyes widening in disbelief, as their ball deviates from its intended path, curving and swerving as if controlled by an invisible hand. These inexplicable phenomena leave golfers scratching their heads, laughing at the whims of fate, and questioning the laws of physics governing the game.

And let us not forget the occasional hazards that lie beneath the surface of the putting green itself. Picture the triumphant golfer, confident in their stroke, only to see their ball encounter an unexpected bump or ridge. The once-smooth green transforms into a playful terrain, conspiring to send balls on thrilling detours or gentle misdirections. It's a spectacle of twists and turns, where even the most meticulously calculated putts succumb to the playful undulations of the green. These unexpected obstacles inject a dose of laughter into the game, reminding us that sometimes, the path to victory is anything but predictable.

As golfers navigate the hazards of the putting green, they learn to embrace the unpredictable, find humor in the unexpected, and cherish the moments of triumph and folly. For in these moments, amidst the buzzing insects, the capricious winds, and the mischievous undulations, lies the essence of the game—a testament to the enduring spirit of resilience, adaptability, and joy that golf embodies.

Unconventional Putting Techniques: In the realm of putting, golfers become visionaries, willing to embrace unorthodox techniques in their relentless pursuit of mastery. Prepare to be entertained as we delve into the colorful world of unconventional putting techniques, where creativity meets hilarity on the greens.

Picture this: a golfer, driven by an insatiable desire to sink every putt, decides to abandon traditional stances in favor of an unorthodox approach. We regale you with tales of golfers contorting their bodies into positions that seem more suited for a yoga class than a golf course. Witness the intrepid golfer who attempts to putt with one leg raised high in the air, convinced that this display of balance will somehow guide the ball to the hole with unparalleled precision. Or perhaps you'll chuckle at the golfer who experiments with putting while standing on one foot, hoping to tap into some hidden well of Zen-like concentration.

But it's not just the stances that bring laughter to the putting green. The gripping tales we have to share will leave you in stitches. Discover the golfer who, in a moment of genius (or madness), decides to grip the putter with their feet, believing that a touch of toe finesse will unlock the secrets of a flawless stroke. Imagine the sight of a golfer attempting to putt with their eyes closed, trusting their instincts and the divine guidance of the golfing gods to lead the ball into the awaiting cup. These unconventional grips may raise a few eyebrows, but they undoubtedly inject a dose of humorous desperation into the game.

And let's not forget the rituals and superstitions that grace the world of putting. From the golfer who insists on whispering sweet nothings to their putter before each stroke, to the one who has an elaborate routine involving spins, hops, and even a few twirls of the putter, putting rituals can border on the absurd. We uncover the tales of golfers who meticulously align their ball with the North Star, convinced that cosmic alignment is the key to sinking every putt. And who could forget the golfer who, upon reaching the green, performs an intricate dance routine that would put a prima ballerina to shame? Whether these rituals bring luck or simply serve as an amusing sideshow, they add an extra layer of intrigue to the art of putting.

In the world of golf, where rules and traditions hold sway, it is the brave souls who dare to defy convention that provide us with endless entertainment. These tales of unconventional putting techniques are not only a testament to the inventive spirit of golfers, but also a reminder that laughter and experimentation have a rightful place on the putting green.

The Saga of the Tricky Breaks: Ah, the dreaded breaks on the green, those mischievous undulations that transform well-intentioned putts into moments of pure hilarity. The battle between golfer and green has raged since time immemorial, and in we regale you with stories that reveal the whimsical nature of these tricky breaks. Prepare to witness the dance of hope and despair as golfers meticulously analyze the undulating terrain, only to have their carefully calculated putts defy gravity and embark on a joyride of their own.

Picture this: a golfer stands before a seemingly innocuous putt, his eyes narrowing as he studies the green like a seasoned detective hunting for clues.

He gauges the slope, considers the speed, and carefully visualizes the perfect line. Confident in his assessment, he strikes the ball with precision, only to watch in awe as it defies all logic, takes an unexpected turn, and meanders off course like a mischievous sprite. Laughter echoes across the green as fellow golfers, with a mix of empathy and amusement, share in the absurdity of the situation.

In "The Saga of the Tricky Breaks," we uncover the art of reading the green—a delicate dance between golfer and the topography beneath their feet. These tales remind us that, despite the meticulous analysis and confident predictions, the green has a sense of humor all its own. It delights in challenging even the most seasoned golfers, playfully defying their expectations and transforming straightforward putts into a tangled web of surprises.

We recount the legendary tales of golfers who believed they had unraveled the secrets of the green, only to have their confidence shattered with each unexpected twist and turn. These stories highlight the universal truth of golf: that even the best-laid plans can go awry, and that sometimes, it's the unexpected moments that bring the most joy.

Imagine the camaraderie that arises as golfers share their experiences of attempting to conquer the enigmatic breaks. They exchange knowing glances and nod in understanding, forming a silent bond of camaraderie. The green becomes a stage for laughter and banter, where each golfer, with a twinkle in their eye, trades tales of putts that defied logic and ended up in inexplicable destinations. It is a shared experience, a testament to the unpredictable nature of the game and the unyielding spirit of those who dare to challenge it.

The Case of the Unpredictable Weather - Nature's Comedy on the Green: Putting—the delicate dance between golfer and green—is a pursuit of precision and finesse. But just when golfers think they have mastered the art, Mother Nature, with her mischievous sense of humor, decides to join in on the fun. We unveil the uproarious encounters that unfold when weather conditions conspire to throw golfers off their game, leaving them both bewildered and amused. Get ready for a whirlwind of comedic weather-related hijinks that will have you laughing till your sides ache and appreciating the unpredictable nature of the game.

Golfers step up to the green, their gaze fixed on the flag, their putters poised for that perfect stroke. Suddenly, a gust of wind swoops down from the heavens, as if sent by mischievous golfing gods, and sends their carefully calculated putt veering off course. Their faces contort in disbelief, their balls swerve like drunken sailors, and the once serene green becomes a stage for wind-induced slapstick comedy. Golfers watch with a mix of frustration and amusement as their putts are transformed into unexpected roller coaster rides, zigzagging across the green like lost souls in search of redemption.

But it's not just wind that adds a challenge to the game. Rain showers, those unexpected guests at the golfing party, arrive unannounced, transforming the meticulously manicured green into a miniature water park. Golfers, determined to soldier on through the deluge, find themselves tiptoeing through puddles, their shoes squelching with each step. As they line up their putts, raindrops fall from above like mischievous sprites, creating a game of aquatic roulette. Will the ball skim gracefully across the water's surface or sink beneath the watery depths? It's a gamble that leaves golfers equal parts perplexed and entertained, their strokes imbued with an unexpected element of aquatic whimsy.

And let us not forget the peculiar dance of golfers attempting to shield themselves from the capricious elements. Umbrellas, once dignified protectors against the rain, take on a life of their own, seemingly possessed by a rebellious spirit. Golfers grapple with these unruly contraptions, fighting against gusts of wind that turn umbrellas inside out or whisk them away like runaway kites. It becomes a spectacle of epic proportions, a battle between golfers and their obstinate umbrellas, where victory is measured by the ability to maintain both dignity and dryness.

As golfers find themselves at the mercy of unpredictable weather, laughter becomes the saving grace amidst the challenging conditions. Frustration gives way to camaraderie as golfers share knowing smiles, recognizing the shared experience of battling the elements. In these moments, the game transcends its competitive nature, becoming a delightful theater of laughter and camaraderie.

So, the next time you step onto the green and a gust of wind taunts your putt or raindrops playfully dance upon the fairways, remember to embrace the unpredictable comedy that Mother Nature has woven into the fabric of golf.

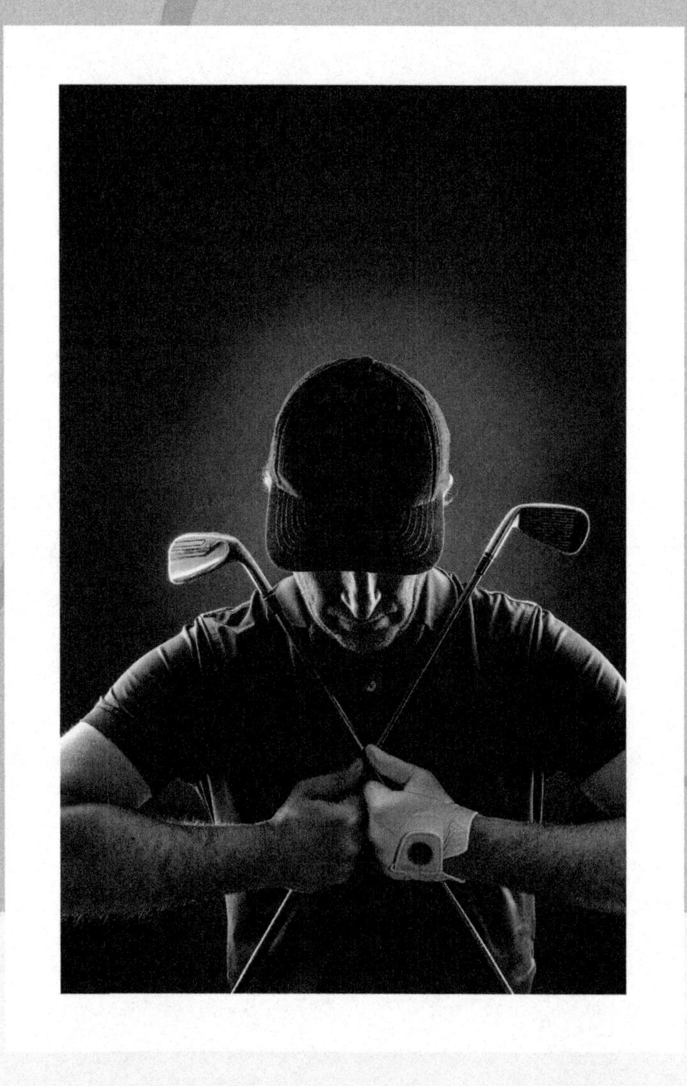

Why am I using a new putter?
Because the old one didn't float too well.

CRAIG STADLER

CHAPTER 10: THE FUNNIEST EXCUSES EVER UTTERED AFTER A GOLF SHOT INTO WATER

"Must have been a mermaid singing sirens from the deep. Mesmerized my ball right into her watery arms."

"That wasn't a shank, it was a strategic "aqua landing" donation to the local fish population. Think of it as underwater philanthropy."

"My club accidentally subscribed to a 'water hazard newsletter.' Now it delivers balls directly to their inbox."

"This is what happens when you try to play golf while simultaneously battling a flock of hungry ducks. They dive-bombed my shot mid-air!"

"Clearly, my ball was tired of the green routine and craved a spa day in the pond. Who am I to deny its hydrotherapy dreams?"

"I think I accidentally hit a golf ball version of the Bermuda Triangle. My shot just vanished into the aquatic abyss."

"That wasn't a shank, it was a 'submarine shot.' Testing out my new underwater golfing technique. Patent pending."

"Fine, you win, pond. But just wait until next time. I'll be back, and I'll bring a snorkel. And maybe a net. And a boat. And... okay, maybe I should just stick to the fairway."

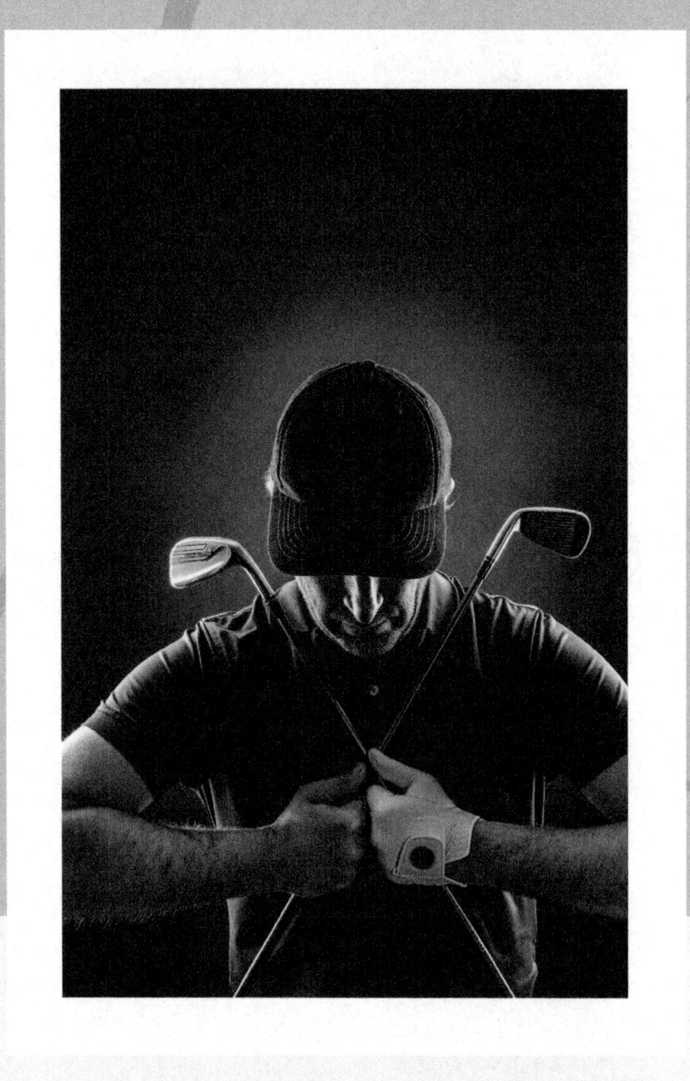

"Golf is a game that's not so much about the ball going where you want it to as it is about not going where you don't want it to."

UNKNOWN

CHAPTER 11: SWING AND MISS: TALES OF GOLFING BLUNDERS AND EPIC FAILS

The Ballad of the Shank - When the Golf Swing Goes Awry: The shank, that dreaded and unpredictable golfing phenomenon, has haunted golfers for generations. It's that moment when the perfect swing takes an unexpected detour, launching the ball in a wild and unintended direction. From fairways to rough, shank shots have produced countless memorable moments on the golf course.

Picture this: A golfer stands confidently on the tee, ready to showcase their skills. The swing begins with precision and promise, but as the club connects with the ball, an unfortunate sound echoes through the air—the dreaded "clank" of a shank. The ball veers sharply to the right, slicing through the fairway like a rogue missile.

In the annals of golfing blunders, there are legendary shank stories that still bring smiles and laughter to the faces of players and spectators alike. There was a time when a prominent golfer, known for their consistency, shanked a shot during a prestigious tournament, leaving everyone in disbelief. The ball ricocheted off a nearby tree, bounced off a golf cart, and ended up in a water hazard, eliciting both gasps and guffaws from the crowd.

But it's not just the professionals who fall victim to the shank's merciless grip. Amateurs and weekend warriors have their fair share of shank tales to tell. From hitting unsuspecting fellow golfers to inadvertently landing in the most inconvenient places, shanked shots have a knack for turning a peaceful round of golf into a comedy of errors.

Oh, the Humanity! Hilarious Tales of Wayward Shots and Missed Targets: The golf course is a theater of humanity's imperfections, where swings can go hilariously awry and targets are missed with remarkable precision. It's in these moments of misfortune that the true essence of the game reveals itself—a shared experience of laughter and camaraderie.

Imagine a golfer attempting a delicate chip shot from the edge of the green, only to see their ball take an unexpected detour. Instead of gracefully rolling towards the pin, it bounces off a rock, sails over a bunker, and ends up nestled comfortably in a spectator's picnic basket. Laughter erupts from the onlookers as the golfer blushes, offering an apologetic wave.

Then there are the instances when golfers mistakenly aim for the wrong target altogether. In a moment of confusion, a player tees off, thinking they're aiming for the fairway, only to realize their ball is soaring towards the adjacent hole. The sudden realization triggers a mix of panic, amusement, and frantic shouts of "Fore!" as golfers from the neighboring fairway scramble to avoid an unexpected aerial assault. These tales of wayward shots and missed targets serve as reminders that golf is not just about precision and technique; it's also about embracing the unpredictable and finding humor in our human foibles. After all, it's the shared laughter and camaraderie born from these moments that make golf such a cherished and enjoyable sport.

As golfers gather around the 19th hole, these stories are shared and retold, perpetuating the folklore of golfing blunders and epic fails. They become part of the tapestry that binds golfers together, reminding us that even the best among us can shank a shot or miss a target. In the world of golf, it's not just about the scorecard—it's about the memories created and the laughter shared along the way. So, the next time you witness a shank or witness a ball take

The Tree Whisperers: Entertaining Encounters with Trees and Foliage: Golfers know all too well that the serene beauty of a golf course can quickly transform into a battleground when they find themselves facing off against the very trees that adorn the fairways. Yes, those leafy sentinels have a mischievous side, ready to wreak havoc on even the most well-intentioned shots. But within these battles against nature, there lies a wellspring of laughter and camaraderie, as golfers share their tales of tree encounters.

One such tale is that of Bob, an avid golfer known for his uncanny ability to find the narrowest gaps between trees. One fateful day, Bob found himself teeing off on a tight par-4 hole, surrounded by a dense forest. With his confidence soaring, he swung with gusto, only to witness his ball ricochet off one tree trunk after another, as if it had developed a personal vendetta against him. Golfers nearby erupted in laughter as Bob's ball finally emerged from the woods, having taken a journey that would make a pinball machine envious.

Another golfing enthusiast, Sarah, had her own unique encounter with nature's obstacles. As she lined up her shot on a picturesque par-3 hole, a gentle breeze whispered through the trees, nudging her ball just off course. Much to her dismay, the ball landed perfectly nestled between two tree roots, defying any chance of a clean shot. Determined not to let nature get the best of her, Sarah attempted a daring low swing, only to witness her ball ricochet off the tree trunk and back towards the tee box. It was a moment that left her fellow golfers doubled over in laughter, and Sarah with a newfound respect for the power of trees.

Indeed, playing from the woods can become a rite of passage for golfers, offering a unique set of challenges and opportunities for hilarity. One particularly memorable instance involved a golfer named Mike, who found his ball lodged high up in a tree's branches. Unwilling to accept defeat, he enlisted the help of his friends and a creative assortment of clubs and contraptions to dislodge the elusive sphere. After several failed attempts, a perfectly timed swing with a long iron sent the ball sailing skyward, only for it to miraculously land back in the same tree. The laughter that erupted on the course that day could be heard for miles.

These stories remind us that golf is not just about perfect shots and low scores; it's about embracing the unexpected and finding joy in the quirks of the game. The trees that line the fairways serve as mischievous co-conspirators, ready to deliver moments of laughter and humility. They teach us the importance of adaptability and the need to laugh at ourselves when the odds are stacked against us. So, the next time your ball disappears into a thicket of trees or you find yourself tangled amidst nature's obstacles, remember that you're not alone. Embrace the challenge, revel in the laughter, and take solace in the fact that you're part of a long-standing tradition of golfers who have encountered the whims of the trees. After all, it's these entertaining encounters that make the game all the more memorable and enjoyable for everyone involved.

Tee Box Terrors: Outrageous Tee Shots and Tee Time Troubles: Golfers often find themselves facing nerve-wracking moments on the tee box, as they prepare to launch their ball down the fairway. However, in the realm of golfing, there are instances where things go hilariously wrong.

These tales of tee shot fiascos and humorous disasters provide endless entertainment and leave players and spectators alike in stitches.

One such unforgettable story involves a golfer, let's call him Matt, who was known for his long, powerful drives off the tee. On this particular day, the wind was howling, and Matt felt compelled to show off his skills. As he teed up his ball and took a mighty swing, he completely missed the ball, sending a spray of grass and dirt flying into the air. The wind, conspiring against him, blew the ball off the tee and onto the nearby cart path. Matt's embarrassment was only matched by the uncontrollable laughter of his playing partners. It was a swing and a miss like no other!

In another tee box tale, we meet Stella, a golfer with a mischievous side. One sunny afternoon, as she stood on the tee box, she noticed a swarm of pesky insects buzzing around her. Not one to be deterred, Stella cleverly devised a plan. With her golf club in hand, she swung at the air, attempting to swat away the insects. Much to her surprise, her club struck the ball perfectly, propelling it straight down the fairway. Stella's unintended trick shot left her fellow golfers astonished and applauding her unorthodox approach to the game.

But tee box terrors aren't limited to human players alone. The animal kingdom has its fair share of memorable moments too. Imagine a peaceful morning on the golf course when a mischievous squirrel decides to make an appearance. As a golfer prepares to tee off, the squirrel scampers onto the tee box and snatches the ball right off the tee, dashing away with it. The golfer is left dumbfounded, while his playing partners erupt in laughter at the squirrel's audacious behavior.

These "fore!"-tunate events on the tee box demonstrate the unpredictable nature of golf and the unexpected moments that can unfold. From swinging and missing the ball entirely to inadvertently achieving incredible shots, the tee box becomes a theater of both triumphs and comical mishaps. It's these moments that keep golfers coming back for more, knowing that no matter how well they prepare, anything can happen when they take their swing.

As golfers continue to tee up their balls and face the challenges of the game, the tee box remains a place of anticipation, nerves, and, most importantly, laughter. The fiascos and disasters that unfold in these moments serve as a reminder that golf is not only a sport of skill but also a playground for unexpected hilarity. So the next time you step onto the tee box, be prepared for anything—and always keep your sense of humor intact. You never know what tee box terrors may lie ahead, ready to create lasting memories and stories that will be shared and cherished for years to come.

"I'm hitting the woods just great, but I'm having a terrible time getting out of them."

HARRY TOFCANO

CHAPTER 12: THE FUNNIEST EXCUSES EVER UTTERED AFTER A GOLF SHOT OUT OF BOUNDS

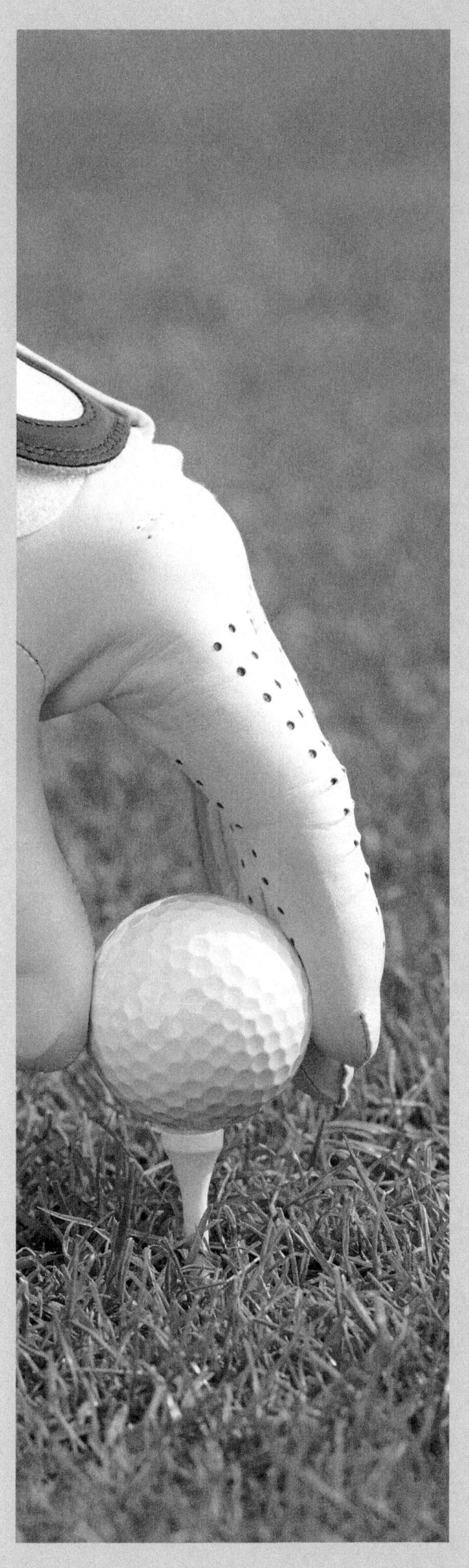

"Must have been abducted by aliens mid-swing. Those little green guys are obsessed with my golf balls, apparently."

"The squirrels staged a coup! They launched a coordinated acorn attack, catapulting my ball into the wilderness."

"Clearly, that fairway boundary line is an optical illusion. My ball saw right through it and went on a solo adventure."

"My swing was so powerful, it created a wormhole on the course. My ball went in, said hi to Stephen Hawking, and came out the other side... lost in the woods."

"My club took artistic license. It interpreted my 'straight down the fairway' request as 'launch it into the unknown.'"

"This is what happens when you try to play golf while simultaneously dodging rogue Frisbees and runaway dogs. Multitasking gone wrong."

"The pressure? What pressure? I thrive under pressure. Like, a lot of pressure. Maybe too much pressure. Okay, maybe that's what sent my ball into orbit."

"Fine, you win, fence. But just wait until next time. I'll be back, and I'll bring a ladder. And maybe a catapult. And a... okay, maybe I should just aim inside the lines."

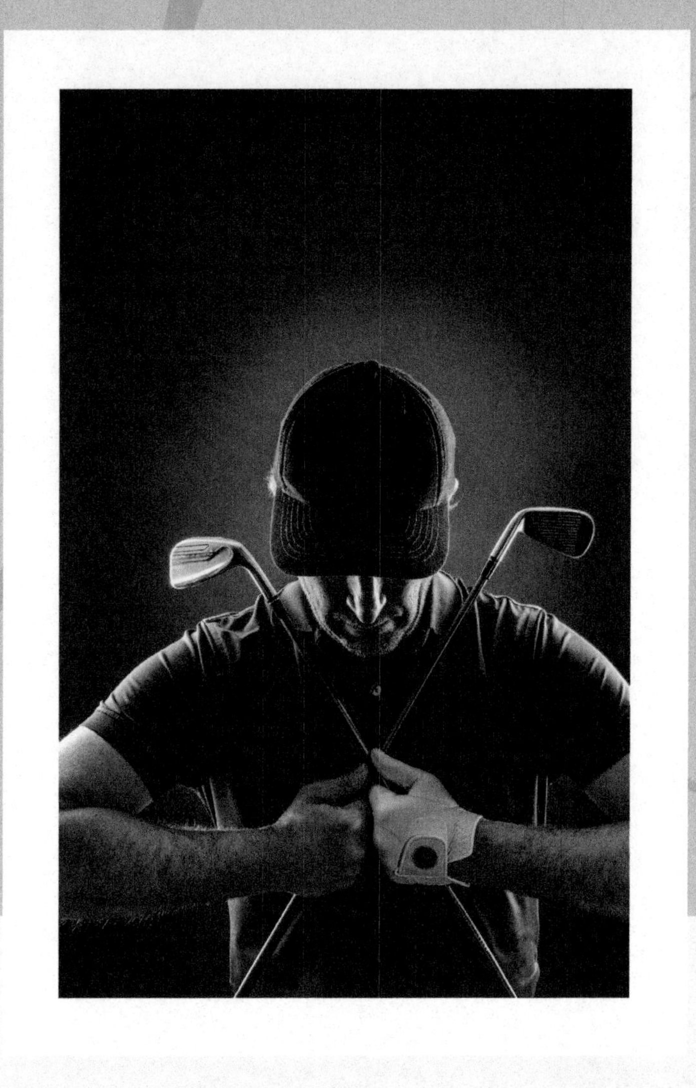

"I'm not saying my golf game went bad, but if I grew tomatoes, they'd come up sliced."

LEE TREVINO

CHAPTER 13: THE UNPREDICTABLE WEATHER: GOLFING IN THE RAIN, WIND, AND MORE

Tales of Golfing in the Rain: Golfing in the rain can be a test of skill, determination, and sometimes, sheer hilarity. As the heavens open up and the fairways transform into waterlogged courses, golfers find themselves facing unexpected challenges and creating unforgettable memories. Let's delve into some humorous anecdotes from those slippery greens and soaked fairways.

Picture this: Golfers dressed head-to-toe in rain gear, wielding umbrellas as if they were shields against the raindrops. The fairways resemble miniature lakes, and the greens become as slick as ice rinks. It's a recipe for laughter and unexpected moments.

In one memorable instance, as a golfer lined up his shot, he carefully positioned himself on the waterlogged fairway. Just as he swung the club, his feet lost traction, causing him to perform an impromptu ice-skating routine. With flailing arms and legs, he slid across the fairway, missing the ball entirely but leaving his fellow golfers in stitches.

Another comical scenario involves the struggle to keep golf equipment dry. Imagine a golfer meticulously wiping his club, ensuring not a drop of rainwater remains. Just as he swings, a rogue gust of wind sends rainwater from a nearby tree cascading down onto his pristine clubface, leaving him with a bewildered expression and a soggy grip.

Umbrella Mishaps and Wet Wedges: Humorous Moments in Wet Weather: Umbrellas, those trusty companions in rainy weather, can turn into unexpected sources of laughter on the golf course. Golfers battling the rain often find themselves grappling with unruly umbrellas, leading to amusing mishaps and wet wedges.

In one amusing incident, a group of golfers took shelter under a large golf umbrella during a sudden downpour. As they huddled close together, trying to stay dry, a particularly strong gust of wind caught the umbrella and lifted it off the ground, taking the golfers along for the ride. They clung to the umbrella for dear life as it whisked them across the fairway, drawing both laughter and bewildered stares from onlookers.

Wet wedges are also a common occurrence during rainy rounds. As golfers attempt to chip onto water-soaked greens, they discover that the ground has turned into a mud bath. In a slapstick fashion, some shots result in mud splatters, covering the golfer's face or even their playing partners. These unexpected "facial masks" of mud never fail to elicit laughter and add a touch of comedy to an otherwise challenging game.

Golfing in the rain may test the resolve of even the most seasoned players, but it also provides a stage for laughter and memorable moments. Slippery greens, soggy fairways, umbrella escapades, and wet wedges create a comedic backdrop that reminds golfers to embrace the lighter side of the game, no matter the weather conditions.

The Great Windy Swing: Golfers often encounter unpredictable weather conditions on the course, and one of the most challenging scenarios is playing in strong winds. The combination of gusts and zephyrs can turn a routine round of golf into a hilarious adventure. From the tee box to the green, the wind can wreak havoc on shots, leading to some truly amusing and memorable moments.

Picture this: a golfer lines up for a drive, feeling confident about their swing. They take a deep breath, envisioning the perfect shot. But just as they begin their backswing, a sudden gust of wind comes out of nowhere, completely altering the trajectory of the ball. Instead of a powerful drive down the fairway, the ball veers off to the side, narrowly missing a group of bewildered fellow golfers. Laughter erupts as everyone realizes the comical nature of the unpredictable wind.

In blustery conditions, even the most experienced golfers can find themselves struggling to maintain control of their shots. The wind becomes a mischievous partner on the course, playing tricks and adding an extra layer of challenge to the game. Golfers watch in awe as their carefully aimed approach shot gets caught in a gust, soaring high above the green and landing in a completely different area. It's not uncommon to hear a chorus of "Did you see that?" and hearty laughter from fellow players witnessing these unexpected outcomes.

Of course, the wind's mischievous nature doesn't stop at altering the trajectory of the ball. It has a way of creating chaos and amusing mishaps. For instance, golfers wearing visors or caps become victims of the wind's capricious whims. One moment, their hat is securely fastened on their head, and the next, a gust comes along, snatching it away like a mischievous prankster. Cue the laughter as the golfer chases after their hat, trying to retrieve it from a nearby pond or shrub.

But it's not just hats that go astray in the wind. Golfers may also find their divots taking flight. As they swing their club into the grass, the gusts catch the displaced turf, transforming it into a temporary airborne spectacle. Imagine the sight of divots soaring through the air like miniature grassy UFOs, eliciting both surprise and amusement from everyone on the course. It's these unexpected moments that make golfing in windy conditions so entertaining.

Moreover, the wind adds an element of uncertainty to putting, often leaving golfers scratching their heads. As they carefully line up their putt, taking into account the green's slope and distance, a sudden gust can intervene, causing the ball to wobble and deviate from its intended path. The ball may roll tantalizingly close to the cup, only to be blown away at the last moment, leaving the golfer in disbelief and their playing partners in fits of laughter.

In the face of these windy challenges, golfers learn to adapt and find humor in the unpredictable nature of the game. They embrace the challenges presented by blustery conditions, turning potential frustrations into shared laughter and camaraderie. Golfers bond over their shared experiences, recounting stories of lost hats, flying divots, and putts that took an unexpected detour.

The great windy swing, with its unexpected outcomes and hilarious moments, becomes a memorable chapter in every golfer's story. Despite the challenges brought by gusts and zephyrs, golfers continue to embrace the game and its unpredictable nature. After all, it's the laughter and the ability to find joy in the midst of windy whimsies that make golf a truly unique and unforgettable sport.

It's during these blustery rounds that golfers truly appreciate the lightheartedness and camaraderie that the game fosters. As they trudge through the course, battling against the wind and sharing in each other's misadventures, friendships are forged and memories are made. The shared laughter becomes a testament to the enduring spirit of the game, where the joy of playing far outweighs any challenges faced along the way.

And let's not forget the creative solutions that golfers come up with in the face of the wind's unpredictable nature. When confronted with a particularly strong gust, some golfers have been known to alter their swing entirely, adopting unorthodox techniques to counter the wind's influence. Picture a golfer performing a windmill-like swing, hoping to harness the power of the gusts and send the ball soaring straight and true. While these improvised swings may not always yield the desired results, they never fail to bring about laughter and amusement among both the golfer and their fellow players.

The windy golf rounds also serve as an opportunity to showcase the lighter side of the game's etiquette. Traditionally, golfers are expected to maintain decorum and composure, but in the face of strong winds, the rules tend to be relaxed, and a more jovial atmosphere takes over. Golfers cheer each other on, applauding particularly impressive shots that managed to defy the wind's influence. They offer playful banter and witty remarks, turning a challenging round into a social event filled with laughter and camaraderie.

Lost hats and flying divots become the stuff of legends on these windy days. Golfers, who might otherwise take themselves too seriously, find themselves humbled by the whimsical nature of the wind. It's a reminder that even in the face of the elements, a sense of humor and a willingness to adapt can make the game all the more enjoyable.

As the winds die down and the round comes to an end, golfers gather in the clubhouse, sharing stories of their wind-blown adventures. These tales become part of the collective lore of the course, passed down from one generation of golfers to the next. They serve as a reminder that in the world of golf, it's not just about the perfect swing or the lowest score; it's about the laughter, the camaraderie, and the ability to find joy in the unexpected.

So, the next time you find yourself on a blustery day at the golf course, don't let the wind deter you. Embrace the challenge it brings, laugh in the face of lost hats and flying divots, and relish in the camaraderie that comes from sharing a round with fellow golfers. Remember, the great windy swing is not just about the shots you make; it's about the memories you create and the stories you'll tell for years to come.

In the unpredictable weather of the golf course, there is always room for laughter and joy. So, let the wind be your companion and the source of mirth, as you navigate the challenges and create unforgettable moments on the greens. After all, golf is not just a game of skill; it's a tapestry of humorous anecdotes, and the wind is but one thread in its rich fabric of amusement.

Navigating Stormy Weather: When dark clouds gather and thunder rumbles in the distance, golfers find themselves caught in the unpredictable grip of a thunderstorm. But amid the stormy chaos, there's room for laughter and lightheartedness. Golfers often showcase their creativity in seeking shelter from the raging elements, resulting in some truly comic escapades.

Picture a group of golfers huddled together under the smallest tree on the course, their golf bags precariously propped against branches to shield them from the downpour. As raindrops fall around them, they exchange jokes and stories, making the most of an otherwise dreary situation. These impromptu sheltering solutions become the source of amusing anecdotes shared and cherished among golfers.

In another instance, a group of golfers, caught in the middle of a sudden thunderstorm, spots a nearby maintenance shed. Eager to escape the rain, they hurriedly take refuge inside. But the small space soon becomes crowded, and their golf bags, dripping wet, make for slippery footing. Laughter erupts as they jostle for space, their rain-soaked clothes and muddy shoes leaving their mark on the shed's interior. It's these moments of shared camaraderie and laughter that make even the most drenched golf rounds memorable.

Amusing Anecdotes of Golfers and Lightning: Lightning can strike fear into the hearts of even the most seasoned golfers, but it also presents opportunities for amusing anecdotes.

Picture a golfer about to tee off on a par 3 hole, blissfully unaware of the approaching storm. Just as he takes his backswing, a brilliant flash of lightning illuminates the sky, followed by a deafening clap of thunder. The golfer jumps, his swing disrupted, and the ball dribbles off the tee, barely reaching a few yards. The combination of startled surprise and lackluster shot leads to uproarious laughter from his fellow players.

Golfers also showcase their creativity when it comes to avoiding lightning strikes. In one instance, a group of golfers uses their golf umbrellas as makeshift lightning rods, believing that their metal-tipped umbrellas will attract lightning away from them. As they huddle together, umbrellas pointed skyward, they jokingly call themselves the "Thunderstorm Deflection Brigade." The sight of golfers standing defiantly under their umbrellas, daring the lightning to strike, draws chuckles and bemusement from others on the course.

Even the golf course itself can play a part in these lightning-laden tales. Imagine a group of golfers seeking shelter in the club's gazebo, only to discover that it's positioned on top of a small hill, making it the highest point around. As they nervously eye the flashing bolts in the distance, they exchange nervous glances and jokes about their choice of shelter. The irony of their situation adds a touch of comedy to the thunderous atmosphere.

In the end, navigating stormy weather on the golf course is not just about avoiding hazards and seeking shelter; it's about finding humor in the face of nature's fury. Golfers bond over shared experiences, trading tales of thunderstorms and lightning strikes, turning potentially harrowing situations into enduring memories filled with laughter.

As the rain pours and thunder rolls, golfers find solace in the camaraderie and comic relief that stormy weather brings. It's in these moments, seeking shelter and exchanging jokes, that the true spirit of golf shines through. The next time a storm disrupts your golf game, remember to embrace the thunderous chuckles and find joy in the unexpected humor that arises. After all, these stories of seeking shelter, laughing in the face of lightning, and creating makeshift solutions become cherished parts of the golfing experience.

One such memorable tale involves a golfer who, in the midst of a thunderstorm, seeks refuge under a conveniently placed picnic table near the ninth hole. As he crouches beneath the table, trying to shield himself from the rain, his fellow golfers join him, forming an impromptu "picnic party" in the pouring rain. They laugh and joke about their unique dining experience, using their golf clubs as utensils and rain-soaked scorecards as makeshift menus. Despite the drenched conditions, their spirits remain high, and they continue their round with renewed energy, relishing the comical bond forged under that picnic table.

The element of surprise also adds an extra layer of amusement to these stormy golfing adventures. Imagine a golfer, focused on his shot, when a sudden crack of thunder startles him. In his moment of surprise, he inadvertently sends the ball flying in the wrong direction, completely missing the fairway. The unexpected diversion leads to laughter from his playing partners, who cheerfully tease him about his "thunder-assisted" shot. It's these unexpected and hilarious moments that make golfing in stormy weather all the more memorable.

Moreover, the unique circumstances of playing golf in inclement weather often bring out the resourcefulness and creativity of golfers. They find inventive ways to protect their equipment and themselves from the rain and lightning. Golf bags become makeshift raincoats, and towels transform into impromptu umbrellas. Golfers fashion waterproof covers for their clubs out of plastic bags, giving rise to the "fashion-forward" golf bag accessories. These ingenious solutions not only offer protection but also provide comedic relief as golfers embrace their improvisational skills.

Golfers also develop their own rituals and superstitions when it comes to playing in stormy conditions. Some may carry lucky charms or engage in peculiar rituals, believing they can ward off lightning strikes or influence the weather. These quirky habits and beliefs become part of the folklore of the golfing community, shared and chuckled over during rainy-day rounds. From wearing mismatched socks to reciting humorous rhymes, golfers find solace in these whimsical practices, adding an element of charm to their stormy golfing adventures.

As the storm clouds eventually disperse and the sun peeks through, golfers emerge from their shelters, their spirits lifted, and their laughter echoing across the greens. They continue their round with a renewed sense of camaraderie and appreciation for the shared experiences that unite them.

In the end, navigating stormy weather on the golf course becomes more than just enduring rain and thunder. It becomes an opportunity for golfers to showcase their resilience, creativity, and sense of humor. The unpredictable weather adds an exciting twist to the game, creating memories that will be retold and cherished for years to come. So, the next time you find yourself caught in a thunderstorm on the golf course, remember to embrace the lightning strikes and thunderous chuckles, for within those moments lies the essence of golf's enduring spirit.

Golf Ball-Sized Hailstones: Hailstorms can be a golfer's worst nightmare, turning a peaceful day on the course into a hilarious and chaotic adventure. Picture this: You're teeing off, enjoying a beautiful round of golf, when suddenly, the sky darkens, and hailstones start pelting down from above. These aren't just any hailstones; they're golf ball-sized monsters, causing panic and amusement in equal measure. As golfers scramble for cover, the absurdity of the situation begins to sink in. Players start taking cover behind golf carts, hiding beneath umbrellas, and even using golf bags as makeshift shields against the relentless onslaught of icy projectiles. It's a comical sight to behold, as golfers frantically dodge hailstones, their swings forgotten in the chaos.

Amidst the chaos, laughter echoes across the fairway. Golfers find themselves exchanging incredulous glances and trading stories of near misses and improvised hailstone dodging techniques. One golfer, who shall forever be known as "The Human Turtle," found ingenious use for his golf bag. He quickly flipped it upside down, creating a makeshift shell that protected him from the unforgiving hail. His resourcefulness became an inspiration for others, who started experimenting with various makeshift shelters and protective gear.

The humor doesn't end there. Picture a golfer, mid-swing, when a particularly large hailstone strikes his golf ball, sending it flying off course. With a mix of disbelief and amusement, he watches as his ball sails high into the air, carried by the power of nature's whims. It becomes a running joke among golfers, a testament to the unpredictable nature of the game and the weather.

But let's not forget the laments. The sound of hailstones pounding on the golf course can be unnerving, turning a serene landscape into a battlefield. Divots are torn from the ground, leaving behind craters resembling lunar landscapes. And for those unfortunate enough to be caught in the open, the hailstones leave their mark, resulting in colorful welts and bruises that become badges of honor.

As the hailstorm subsides, golfers emerge from their makeshift shelters, a mixture of relief, laughter, and a newfound camaraderie. They may be soaking wet, bruised, and their golf game in shambles, but they've experienced something unique, something that will be shared and retold for years to come.

Fun and Frolics on Snow-Covered Courses: As the temperature drops and winter blankets the golf courses in a pristine layer of snow, golfers don't let the cold weather dampen their spirits. Instead, they embrace the opportunity for unique and amusing wintertime golfing adventures. One of the most beloved activities among winter golf enthusiasts is the snowball golf match.

Picture a group of golfers equipped with their trusty golf clubs, trudging through the snow-covered fairways, leaving trails of footprints behind them. The golf balls are replaced with snowballs, meticulously shaped and compacted for optimal aerodynamics (or at least as close to optimal as a snowball can get). The objective? To navigate the snow-laden course, avoiding snowdrift hazards and aiming for makeshift targets amidst the winter wonderland.

With snowballs in hand, the golfers take their positions, ready to tee off with a comical twist. Laughter echoes across the snow-covered fairways as they attempt to launch their snowballs into the air, hoping for a decent distance and a semblance of accuracy. Of course, the unpredictability of snowball flight ensures plenty of hilarity, as some shots veer wildly off course or disintegrate mid-air in a burst of powdery snow.

The competitive spirit is alive and well, but with a playful twist. Instead of counting strokes, players measure success by the distance their snowballs travel or by the number of successful hits on their targets. It's all about embracing the wintry conditions and reveling in the camaraderie that comes with shared laughter and good-natured banter.

Snowball golf matches often come with their fair share of unexpected challenges. Aiming for a target obscured by snowdrifts can lead to wild miscalculations, resulting in snowballs soaring high over their intended mark or barely rolling a few feet. The unpredictability of the terrain adds an extra layer of excitement, with golfers sliding and slipping on icy patches, occasionally tumbling into soft snowbanks. These amusing tumbles and slips often elicit uproarious laughter, turning the game into a lighthearted winter spectacle.

Of course, the fun doesn't end at the tee. As players traverse the frosty greens and icy fairways, they encounter unique obstacles that only winter golf can provide.

Frozen ponds, once tranquil water hazards, now serve as a source of entertainment. Golfers test their luck and skill by attempting to skip their snowballs across the frozen surface, hoping for a perfect ricochet or a dramatic splash. Needless to say, not all attempts go as planned, and icy mishaps become a common occurrence, leaving the players in fits of laughter.

The greens themselves, usually a smooth carpet of grass, transform into a challenging terrain of frozen undulations. Putting becomes an exercise in precision and patience, as the golfers navigate the icy slopes and unexpected bumps. A seemingly straightforward putt can turn into a hilarious adventure, with the snowball taking unexpected detours or stubbornly refusing to reach its intended destination. It's a true test of adaptability and a reminder that even in wintertime, golf can be a delightfully unpredictable game.

In the realm of snowball golf matches and frosty fairways, the scorecard becomes a secondary concern. The real victory lies in the shared joy, the laughter echoing through the winter air, and the memories forged in the midst of unconventional golfing adventures.

These wintertime golfing escapades serve as a reminder that the spirit of golf transcends seasons, and even in the coldest of conditions, a little creativity and a lot of laughter can turn a round of golf into an unforgettable experience.

So, whether it's launching snowballs into the air, sliding across icy fairways, or attempting daring shots across frozen ponds, wintertime golfing adventures offer a unique blend of challenge and amusement. Golfers find themselves embracing the real nature of sport amidst the winter landscape, fostering a sense of camaraderie and shared merriment.

Snowball golf matches and the accompanying hilarity that ensues bring golfers together in a way that transcends the usual competitive nature of the game. It's not about who wins or loses, but rather about the shared experiences and the bonds formed over shared laughter and good-natured teasing. These winter golfing adventures create lasting memories and stories that are passed down from one season to the next, strengthening the sense of community among golfers who dare to venture onto the snow-covered courses.

In addition to the joy of snowball golf matches, wintertime golfing also offers a picturesque setting that captivates the senses. The serenity of a snow-covered course, with the sun glistening on the icy landscape, creates a tranquil atmosphere that contrasts with the energetic and laughter-filled moments of the game. Golfers find themselves immersed in a world where the beauty of nature intertwines with the joy of the sport, resulting in a truly enchanting experience.

Of course, wintertime golfing adventures also come with their fair share of practical challenges. Golfers bundle up in layers of warm clothing, donning colorful hats and scarves to brave the chilly temperatures. The sound of clubs striking snowballs mingles with the crunch of footsteps on the icy ground, creating a symphony unique to winter golf. It's a testament to the dedication and passion of golfers who refuse to let a little cold weather keep them away from the game they love.

As the day draws to a close, and the sun begins its descent, golfers gather in the clubhouse, their cheeks rosy from the cold and their hearts warmed by the memories made on the snow-covered fairways. Laughter and animated conversations fill the room as players recount their favorite moments and funny mishaps from the day's golfing adventures. The shared camaraderie and the sense of belonging are palpable, reminding everyone present that golf is more than just a game—it's a community of individuals brought together by their love for the sport and their willingness to embrace the chills of winter.

In the realm of wintertime golfing, where snowball golf matches and frosty greens reign, the focus shifts from technique and scores to laughter and camaraderie. It's a chapter in the book of golf that celebrates the lighthearted side of the sport, reminding us that even in the face of challenging conditions, there's always room for merriment and joy. These wintertime golfing adventures add a touch of magic to the game, infusing it with a playful spirit that keeps golfers coming back for more, season after season.

So, the next time you find yourself surrounded by a snow-covered golf course, don't hesitate to grab your clubs and a few snowballs. Embrace the game you love, laugh in the face of icy challenges, and create memories that will warm your heart long after the winter has passed. Because in the world of wintertime golfing, snow jokes are not just allowed—they're encouraged.

"Sometimes the biggest problem is in your head. You've got to believe."

JACK NICKLAUS

CHAPTER 14: TALES FROM THE 19TH HOLE: HILARIOUS BANTER AND POST-GAME CHATTER

This section takes us into the heart of the golfing community, where the clubhouse serves as a hub for camaraderie, laughter, and memorable conversations. After a challenging round of golf, players gather in the clubhouse to unwind, share their experiences, and relive the highlights and lowlights of their game. It is in these moments that hilarious banter and post-game chatter thrive, creating a vibrant atmosphere filled with laughter and camaraderie.

As golfers settle into comfortable chairs, exchanging stories with their fellow players, the clubhouse comes alive with animated discussions and good-natured ribbing. The tales from the 19th hole often revolve around memorable shots, extraordinary luck, and even unfortunate blunders. These stories are retold with gusto, with each player trying to outdo the others in both wit and humor.

One popular topic of conversation is the spectacular shot that defied all odds. Golfers enthusiastically share their own versions of "once-in-a-lifetime" shots, embellishing the details for comedic effect. Stories of improbable chip-ins, miraculous recoveries from the rough, and long putts sinking against all expectations abound. The players relish the opportunity to showcase their shot-making skills, while injecting humor and exaggeration into their narratives, much to the delight of their audience.

Of course, not all tales revolve around triumph. Golfers also regale each other with humorous stories of mishaps and blunders on the course. From the golfer who mistook their partner's ball for their own, leading to an embarrassing tee shot, to the player who slipped on a banana peel (yes, it happens!) during a crucial swing, these anecdotes provide endless amusement and light-hearted entertainment. The shared experience of golfing misfortunes creates a bond among players, who can find solace in laughter and a shared understanding that golf can be as humbling as it is rewarding.

The 19th hole also serves as a platform for friendly banter and good-natured teasing among golfing buddies. Golfers often engage in playful one-upmanship, challenging each other's skills and playfully mocking their rivals.

It's not uncommon to hear witty remarks about missed putts, wayward drives, or a player's peculiar swing technique. These lighthearted jabs are delivered with affection, fostering a sense of camaraderie and adding to the jovial atmosphere of the clubhouse.

One of the joys of the 19th hole banter is the opportunity to reminisce about past rounds and legendary golfing moments. Players recount memorable shots from their own experiences or famous shots witnessed in tournaments. These stories become larger than life, with every retelling adding a touch of flair and amusement. Tales of extraordinary comebacks, improbable victories, and hilarious on-course encounters become the stuff of legend within the golfing community.

The 19th hole conversations are not limited to personal experiences alone. Golfers also enjoy discussing the latest golf news, debating the performances of professional golfers, and speculating on upcoming tournaments. These discussions provide an opportunity to share insights, exchange opinions, and engage in friendly banter about the sport they love. From analyzing swing techniques to predicting the outcome of major championships, these conversations fuel the passion and enthusiasm for golf among the players.

In addition to the spoken word, the 19th hole banter often includes playful gestures and humorous rituals. It is not uncommon to witness mock award ceremonies, where players present comical trophies for various achievements, such as the "most creative excuse for a bad shot" or the "most persistent bunker magnet." These light-hearted rituals further strengthen the bond among golfers and create cherished memories that go beyond the game itself

This section takes us into the realm of the clubhouse, where golfers gather after their rounds to relax, share stories, and enjoy each other's company. The clubhouse is a melting pot of personalities, and it's in this vibrant setting that golfers often encounter eccentric individuals who leave a lasting impression. These encounters not only add to the amusement and enjoyment of the game but also create unforgettable memories that are shared and cherished by golfers for years to come.

One of the most remarkable characters you might meet in the clubhouse is the eccentric member with a unique golfing superstition. Every golf club seems to have at least one of these individuals whose quirky beliefs and rituals become legendary among fellow golfers. Picture a golfer meticulously arranging their golf balls in a specific pattern before every shot, firmly convinced that it enhances their luck. Or perhaps there's a member who insists on wearing mismatched socks because they believe it brings them good fortune on the course. The clubhouse buzzes with laughter and curiosity as these eccentric personalities share their beliefs, captivating everyone with their dedication to these unusual superstitions.

Another fascinating character you might encounter is the charismatic golf pro with a flair for storytelling. These professionals not only possess exceptional golfing skills but also have the ability to entertain with their tales and anecdotes. Picture a pro regaling a group of captivated listeners with humorous accounts of their adventures on the golf circuit, sharing behind-the-scenes mishaps and the camaraderie among fellow players. Their larger-than-life personalities and knack for storytelling transform the clubhouse into a theater of laughter and entertainment. Golfers eagerly gather around, hanging onto every word, as the golf pro weaves captivating narratives that transport them to the world of professional golf.

But it's not just the members and professionals who bring color to the clubhouse; the staff members also contribute to the tapestry of eccentric personalities. From the cheerful bartender who knows everyone's favorite drink to the meticulous locker room attendant who always has a witty remark, the clubhouse staff play an integral role in creating a welcoming and jovial atmosphere. These individuals become familiar faces and develop unique relationships with the golfers, often sharing humorous banter and inside jokes. Their presence adds an extra layer of warmth and character to the clubhouse experience, making it a place where golfers feel not only like members but also like part of a close-knit community.

In the realm of the clubhouse, chance encounters with fellow golfers can lead to unforgettable exchanges. It's not uncommon to strike up a conversation with someone you've never met before, only to discover a shared passion for the game and a natural camaraderie.

These encounters can range from the humorous to the heartwarming, as golfers bond over their shared experiences and love for the sport. From trading funny anecdotes about memorable shots to engaging in friendly debates about golfing techniques, these conversations foster a sense of belonging and create lasting connections.

The clubhouse becomes a microcosm of the golfing world, where golfers from different backgrounds and walks of life come together, united by their love for the game. It's a place where laughter echoes through the air, where stories are shared and cherished, and where friendships are forged over a shared passion. The characters you meet in the clubhouse leave an indelible mark on your golfing journey, infusing it with joy, humor, and a sense of community.

As you walk into the clubhouse after a round of golf, be prepared to encounter an array of eccentric personalities who will both entertain and enrich your experience. From the superstitious golfer with their peculiar rituals to the golf pro who mesmerizes with their tales, these characters add an extra dimension to the game. Embrace the lively atmosphere, engage in conversations, and immerse yourself in the fascinating stories and encounters that unfold within the clubhouse walls.

The clubhouse is a place where laughter flows freely, where jokes are shared, and where the camaraderie among golfers blossoms. It's a setting that embodies the spirit of the game, where the love for golf unites individuals from all walks of life. Within these walls, time seems to stand still as golfers gather to relish the moments of victory, commiserate over missed shots, and celebrate the bonds forged through their shared passion.

As you engage with the characters you meet in the clubhouse, you'll come to appreciate the true essence of golf. It's not just about swinging clubs and chasing a little white ball; it's about the human connections and the stories that unfold along the way. The eccentric personalities you encounter remind you that golf is not only a game of skill but also a stage for self-expression and individuality.

Through these encounters, you'll come to realize that the clubhouse is not just a physical space; it's a sanctuary where golfers find solace, create lasting memories, and share in the joys and challenges of the game. The characters you meet will stay with you long after you leave the clubhouse, serving as a reminder of the laughter, camaraderie, and the enduring spirit of golf.

The locker room is not just a place to change clothes and store golf gear; it's also a hub of camaraderie and laughter. Within the locker room's hallowed walls, golfers from all walks of life come together to share jokes, play pranks, and enjoy light-hearted moments that add a touch of mirth to their golfing experience.

One of the most common forms of locker room laughter is the exchange of humorous jokes. Golfers love to unleash their wit and engage in banter that tickles the funny bone. nd build relationships.

These jokes often revolve around the peculiarities of the game itself, such as the frustrations of putting or the unpredictability of a golf swing. Here's an example of a classic golf joke that often circulates in locker rooms:

"Why don't golfers ever get married? Because they can't find anyone who can match their handicap!"

Such jokes bring smiles to the faces of golfers, as they find solace and shared experiences in the laughter that ensues. The locker room becomes a safe space where golfers can bond through humor, using jokes as a way to connect and build relationships.

Beyond jokes, playful pranks are another hallmark of locker room laughter. Golfers often find creative ways to lighten the mood and catch their fellow players off guard. One common prank involves swapping clubs or hiding them in unexpected places. Imagine the laughter that erupts when a golfer reaches into their bag only to find their driver replaced with a putter or discovers their irons mysteriously hidden in the ceiling tiles!

Of course, pranks must be executed with a sense of camaraderie and respect, ensuring that they remain lighthearted and harmless. Golfers understand the unwritten code that governs pranks, emphasizing the importance of good-natured fun and mutual enjoyment.

It's not just jokes and pranks that generate locker room laughter. Light-hearted moments also play a significant role in creating an atmosphere of joy and camaraderie. Golfers often share amusing stories of their on-course adventures or recount comical encounters with wildlife on the fairway. These tales become legendary within the golfing community and are passed down from generation to generation, becoming part of the rich tapestry of golfing lore.

In addition to stories, the locker room is a space where golfers can let their guard down and be themselves. They can talk about their golfing successes and failures, recounting the shots that made them feel like pros or sharing tales of their most spectacular mishits. These moments of vulnerability and shared experiences create a sense of unity among golfers, fostering an environment where laughter and support thrive.

Furthermore, the locker room is not limited to the professionals or seasoned golfers; it is a place where players of all skill levels can come together. Novices can seek guidance and advice from more experienced golfers, leading to humorous exchanges and light-hearted moments as they navigate the complexities of the game.

The locker room laughter extends beyond the confines of the physical space. It becomes a bond that golfers carry with them onto the course, creating a relaxed and enjoyable atmosphere. The shared jokes and pranks act as reminders that golf is not just about the technicalities and the scorecard but also about the friendships forged and the joy found in each swing.

In conclusion, the locker room is a treasure trove of laughter in the world of golf. Within its walls, golfers find solace in humorous jokes, engage in playful pranks, and share light-hearted moments that enhance their overall clubhouse experience. This vibrant atmosphere of camaraderie and mirth is an integral part of the golfing community, fostering a sense of unity and creating memories that will be cherished long after the final putt is sunk.

So, the next time you step into a golf locker room, embrace the laughter and camaraderie that permeates the air. Engage in the exchange of jokes, be open to playful pranks, and relish the light-hearted moments shared with fellow golfers. Remember that while golf may be a serious game, there is always room for laughter and a bit of mischief.

In the end, it's the moments of laughter in the locker room that become cherished memories for golfers. They serve as a reminder that beyond the competitive nature of the sport, there is an underlying joy and sense of community that unites golfers from all walks of life. The locker room becomes a sanctuary where players can momentarily escape the pressures of the game and simply enjoy the lighter side of golf.

As you leave the locker room and step onto the course, carry that laughter with you. Let it fuel your spirit and lighten your swing. Remember that golf is not just about the technical aspects or the pursuit of a perfect score. It's about the connections we make, the bonds we forge, and the moments of shared laughter that make the game truly enjoyable.

So, embrace the locker room laughter, cherish the jokes, pranks, and light-hearted moments. They are the threads that weave together the fabric of the golfing community, creating an atmosphere of warmth, friendship, and endless amusement. And in the end, it is this sense of camaraderie and shared joy that truly makes the game of golf an extraordinary experience.

So, go forth, and let the echoes of laughter resonate on the fairways and greens. May the locker room be a place where you find not only your golf gear but also a sanctuary of mirth and connection. Let the sound of laughter accompany your swings, and remember that in the world of golf, sometimes the best memories are not made from birdies and eagles, but from the smiles and laughter shared along the way.

Clubhouse Confessions: Tales of Embarrassing Moments and Golfing Blunders: Golf, a game often associated with elegance and grace, has a way of humbling even the most skilled players. Within the clubhouse walls, where golfers gather to unwind and share their experiences, tales of embarrassing moments and golfing blunders are exchanged with laughter and camaraderie.

These confessions not only provide entertainment but also remind us that even the best players can find themselves in hilariously awkward situations on the course.

One common source of embarrassment on the golf course is the dreaded case of mistaken identity – hitting the wrong ball. It's a scenario that has played out countless times, causing both amusement and frustration. Picture this: A golfer, lost in the depths of concentration, approaches what they believe to be their ball in the fairway. They confidently swing, only to realize that they have just launched someone else's ball into the distance. The sheer disbelief and subsequent embarrassment make for a humorous story to share in the clubhouse. Such tales serve as a reminder to double-check those ball markings and to always be aware of one's surroundings.

Misreading a putt can also lead to comical moments on the greens. Golfers often find themselves trying to decipher the break and speed of a putt, only to have their calculations go hilariously awry. Picture a golfer lining up what they believe to be a gentle left-to-right break, only to see the ball veer sharply to the right, completely confounding their expectations.

These misreadings can result in exaggerated gestures, like wide-eyed disbelief or even mimicking the path of the ball with outstretched arms, much to the amusement of fellow players. These stories are relatable to golfers of all skill levels, as we've all experienced the frustration of a misread putt at some point.

The stories shared in the clubhouse also serve as a reminder that even professional golfers are not exempt from embarrassing moments. From major championship blunders to televised slip-ups, even the best in the world have experienced their fair share of humbling mishaps. These tales humanize the game and remind golfers that no matter their skill level, everyone is susceptible to the occasional misstep. Whether it's a professional golfer falling victim to a slippery divot on live television or a weekend warrior mistakenly using the wrong club during a friendly tournament, these stories generate a collective sense of understanding and laughter.

The confessions of embarrassing moments and golfing blunders within the clubhouse walls create an environment where golfers can laugh at themselves and find solace in shared experiences.

These stories weave a tapestry of laughter, connecting golfers of all backgrounds and skill levels. The clubhouse becomes a sanctuary where players can shed the pressure of the game and revel in the hilarity that arises from their own mistakes and blunders.

As the evening wears on and the stories continue to flow, the bonds of friendship grow stronger, forged through laughter and the shared understanding that golf is a game meant to be enjoyed, imperfections and all. These confessions serve as a reminder that the true joy of golf lies not just in the pursuit of a perfect swing but also in the ability to laugh at ourselves and embrace the unpredictable and humorous moments that make the game so special. In the end, it's the clubhouse confessions that create lasting memories and remind golfers that the true measure of a round is not solely based on the scorecard but also on the laughter and camaraderie shared with fellow players. These confessions bring levity to the golfing community, fostering a sense of belonging and reminding everyone that they are part of a larger tapestry of golfing experiences.

As the night goes on, the clubhouse becomes a place where stories are embellished, laughter echoes through the halls, and new friendships are forged. The confessions of embarrassing moments and golfing blunders serve as an equalizer, erasing the boundaries of age, skill, and status. In this inclusive atmosphere, golfers find comfort in the fact that even the most celebrated professionals have their share of comical blunders.

The beauty of these confessions lies not only in the amusement they provide but also in their relatability. Every golfer, regardless of skill level, has experienced embarrassing moments on the course. It's the shared understanding of these experiences that strengthens the bond between players and fosters a sense of community.

Within the clubhouse, there is no judgment or ridicule. Instead, there is laughter, support, and the celebration of the human element of golf. Golfers find solace in knowing that they are not alone in their occasional missteps, and that the game itself embraces imperfections with open arms. These confessions help golfers embrace the lighter side of the sport, reminding them that golf is not solely about technique and competition, but also about the joy of the journey and the stories that come along with it.

In the realm of clubhouse confessions, golfers discover the power of self-deprecation and humility. They learn to laugh at their own mistakes and find humor in the unpredictable nature of the game. These confessions become a source of inspiration, encouraging golfers to take risks, let go of perfectionism, and approach the game with a lighthearted mindset.

The tales of embarrassing moments and golfing blunders shared within the clubhouse walls serve as a testament to the enduring spirit of the game. They remind golfers that while the pursuit of excellence is admirable, it's the joy, laughter, and connection with others that truly make the golfing experience memorable.

Of course, clubhouse confessions aren't limited to on-course blunders. Golfers also recount stories of embarrassing moments within the confines of the clubhouse itself. From accidentally walking into the wrong locker room to struggling with the complexities of locker combination locks, these small mishaps can turn into memorable moments of embarrassment. Golfers often find themselves sharing anecdotes of their own foibles, such as mistaking someone else's bag for their own or accidentally wearing mismatched shoes onto the first tee. These tales create a sense of camaraderie among players, as they realize they are not alone in their occasional lapses of judgment or absent-mindedness.

In the spirit of self-deprecation and shared laughter, golfers have embraced the notion that even the most skilled players are bound to make embarrassing blunders. These confessions serve as a reminder that golf is a game where imperfections and mistakes are not only expected but also celebrated. They create an inclusive and light-hearted atmosphere within the golfing community, where golfers can bond over shared experiences and find solace in knowing that their own embarrassing moments are part of a universal tapestry of golfing blunders.

In the spirit of self-deprecation and shared laughter, golfers have embraced the notion that even the most skilled players are bound to make embarrassing blunders. These confessions serve as a reminder that golf is a game where imperfections and mistakes are not only expected but also celebrated. They create an inclusive and light-hearted atmosphere within the golfing community, where golfers can bond over shared experiences and find solace in knowing that their own embarrassing moments are part of a universal tapestry of golfing blunders.

As golfers gather in the clubhouse, the confessions of embarrassing moments and golfing blunders become a cherished part of the post-round ritual. Players take turns recounting their most unforgettable blunders, each story met with laughter and empathetic nods. The stories not only provide entertainment but also foster a sense of camaraderie and a shared understanding that golf is a game that humbles even the most talented players.

One common theme in these confessions is the occasional loss of composure and the resulting comedic mishaps. Picture a golfer who, after a particularly frustrating hole, tosses their club in a fit of exasperation, only to watch in disbelief as it takes an unexpected bounce and ends up in the water hazard. The exaggerated gesture of frustration quickly turns into a moment of self-awareness and laughter, as fellow golfers tease them about their "impressive club toss." These confessions remind us that even the most composed and disciplined players can succumb to the occasional outburst of emotion, resulting in amusing consequences.

Another source of humorous confessions lies in the world of golfing attire. From loud and flamboyant patterns to ill-fitting outfits, golfers have seen it all. There's the tale of the golfer who accidentally wore two different colored socks, only realizing the fashion faux pas when their playing partners couldn't contain their laughter on the first tee. And then there's the golfer who unknowingly left the price tag on their new golf hat, proudly displaying it to the amusement of everyone they encountered on the course. These wardrobe malfunctions add a touch of light-heartedness to the game, reminding golfers that fashion mistakes are all part of the golfing experience.

Clubhouse confessions also shed light on the unique and sometimes perplexing golfing rituals and superstitions that players engage in. Golfers may admit to bizarre pre-shot routines or quirky rituals they believe will bring them luck. For example, one golfer may confess to tapping their club on every tee box for good measure, while another might reveal their unusual lucky charm tucked away in their golf bag. These superstitious habits often spark laughter and friendly banter among players, highlighting the idiosyncrasies that make the game of golf so endearing.

So, as golfers gather in the clubhouse, ready to unwind after a challenging round, the air is filled with anticipation. The confessions begin, and the room is enveloped in laughter, storytelling, and a genuine sense of camaraderie. The clubhouse becomes a sanctuary, a place where golfers can leave their egos at the door and embrace the shared experiences that make the game of golf truly special.

The Wisdom of the 19th Hole: Golfing wisdom and advice is often exchanged among golfers at the 19th hole. As golfers gather in the clubhouse to unwind after a round of golf, the atmosphere becomes ripe for sharing amusing sayings, tongue-in-cheek proverbs, and comical perspectives on the game.

Quirky Sayings: Golf is a sport known for its unique terminology and colorful expressions. At the 19th hole, golfers often share quirky sayings that have been passed down through generations, adding a touch of humor to the conversation. For example, you might hear someone say, "Golf is like a love affair - if you don't take it too seriously, it's a lot more fun!" Such sayings encapsulate the lighthearted nature of the game and remind golfers not to take themselves too seriously.

Tongue-in-Cheek Proverbs: Golfers have a knack for turning traditional proverbs on their heads to create amusing golf-specific versions. These tongue-in-cheek proverbs add a playful twist to the wisdom usually associated with such sayings. For instance, a golfer might say, "A bad day on the golf course beats a good day at work... unless you're a golf pro!" This kind of humor highlights the escapism and joy that golf brings to players, even in the face of challenges.

Comical Golfing Advice: The 19th hole is a breeding ground for comical golfing advice. Whether it's a golfer offering unconventional tips or sharing humorous anecdotes about their own experiences, the advice exchanged in this setting often brings laughter and camaraderie. One might hear advice like, "To improve your swing, just remember: the ball is afraid of heights. So, swing for the moon!" These humorous tips acknowledge the complexities of the game while reminding golfers to find joy in the process rather than obsessing over perfection.

The wisdom and humor shared at the 19th hole are an essential part of the golfing experience. These lighthearted exchanges provide a refreshing contrast to the intense focus required on the course.

Golfers recognize that while the game may present challenges and frustrations, it is also a source of joy, laughter, and endless entertainment.

Legendary Golfing Anecdotes: In addition to sayings and proverbs, the 19th hole is a treasure trove of legendary golfing anecdotes. Golfers love to share stories about incredible shots, miraculous recoveries, and unbelievable occurrences on the course. These anecdotes often take on a comical twist as golfers embellish their tales with humorous details. For instance, you might hear a story about a golfer who managed to hit the ball backward, only for it to bounce off a tree and miraculously land in the hole. These stories bring laughter and entertainment to the clubhouse, showcasing the unpredictable and often absurd nature of the game.

The Joy of Camaraderie: Above all, the conversations at the 19th hole highlight the joy of camaraderie among golfers. As they sit back with a drink in hand, golfers bond over shared experiences, amusing stories, and laughter. The exchange of witty sayings, humorous proverbs, and comical advice serves as a unifying thread, reinforcing the sense of community that exists within the golfing world. It is in these moments that lifelong friendships are formed, and golfers find solace in the shared love for the game.

Golfers understand that while the game demands skill and concentration, it is equally important to embrace the lighter moments and find laughter along the way.

The conversations at the 19th hole not only provide a platform for laughter and amusement but also foster a sense of community among golfers. It is during these moments that bonds are strengthened, friendships are formed, and memories are shared. The shared experiences and shared love for the game create a special connection among golfers, making the 19th hole a place of laughter, relaxation, and connection.

"I believe in positive thinking.
Believing in yourself."

ANNIKA SORENSTAM

CHAPTER 15: BEYOND THE 18TH HOLE

As the sun dips below the horizon, casting a warm glow across the 18th green, we find ourselves standing at the crossroads of reflection and anticipation. The fairways and greens have witnessed our struggles, witnessed the evolution of our swings and the transformation of our perspectives. It's a moment to acknowledge that golf is not just a game; it's a life lesson, an ongoing odyssey.

The pursuit of golfing excellence is not a destination but a perpetual expedition—one marked by peaks and valleys, laughter and introspection. The lessons learned on the course extend beyond swing mechanics and putting techniques. They delve into the realms of patience, resilience, and the joy of embracing imperfections.

As we bid adieu to the book, we do so not with finality but with a newfound understanding. The golf course mirrors life—an unpredictable journey where adaptability is key, and the ability to laugh at our own missteps is a true measure of wisdom. The frustrations we've shared and the triumphs we've celebrated form the mosaic of experiences that shape us.

With a gentle nod to the 18th hole, we carry the stories, laughter, and camaraderie into our future endeavors. The book's purpose transcends its pages; it's a catalyst for personal growth, a reminder that the pursuit of joy is as integral to the game as mastering the swing.

As the closing chapter whispers its final words, the golf bag slung over our shoulder feels lighter, the lessons etched in our memory more profound. We step away from the 18th green not as victors over a game but as enthusiasts of a lifelong journey, ready to face the next challenge with resilience, camaraderie, and an unwavering love for the ultimate game of golf. And so, with a hopeful gaze toward the horizon, we embark on the next chapter, carrying the spirit of the game with us.

CHAPTER 16: GOLF JOKES

"Golfer: 'My golf is awful, I think I'm going to drown myself in the lake.'
Caddy: 'Think you can keep your head down for that long?'"

Golfer: ‘Do you think I can get there with a 5-iron?'
Caddy: ‘Eventually‘

Golfer: ‘You've got to be the worst caddy in the world'
Caddy: ‘Surely not!, that would be too much of a coincidence‘

"Why did Tarzan spend so much time on the golf course?" He was perfecting his swing!

"Why did the golfer wear two pairs of shorts?" In case he got a hole in one!

"How many golfers does it take to change a light bulb? FOUR!

"My friend just collapsed into a display of golf clubs... Paramedics are doing what they can but he's not out of the woods yet!"

"What's the difference between a golfer and a vacuum cleaner? A vacuum cleaner stops sucking when it gets to the hole."

"I finally got a hole-in-one! Too bad it was on the practice green."

"I went to the golf shop for a new putter. The guy said, 'Have you tried aiming better?'"

"The weatherman on TV said there's a 90% chance of rain for today's round. I said, 'Challenge accepted!'"

How does a golfer ensure a good night's sleep?
By putting on his "par"-jamas!

What do you call a group of musical golfers?
A swing band!

"I played a round with a guy who used a compass to aim his shots. He said, 'I'm just following the direction of my dreams."

"Golfer: 'Do you think this club is long enough?'
Caddy: 'Depends. How far are you planning to miss the green by?'"

"Golf is the only sport where you can spend all day outside and still come home smelling like a bar."

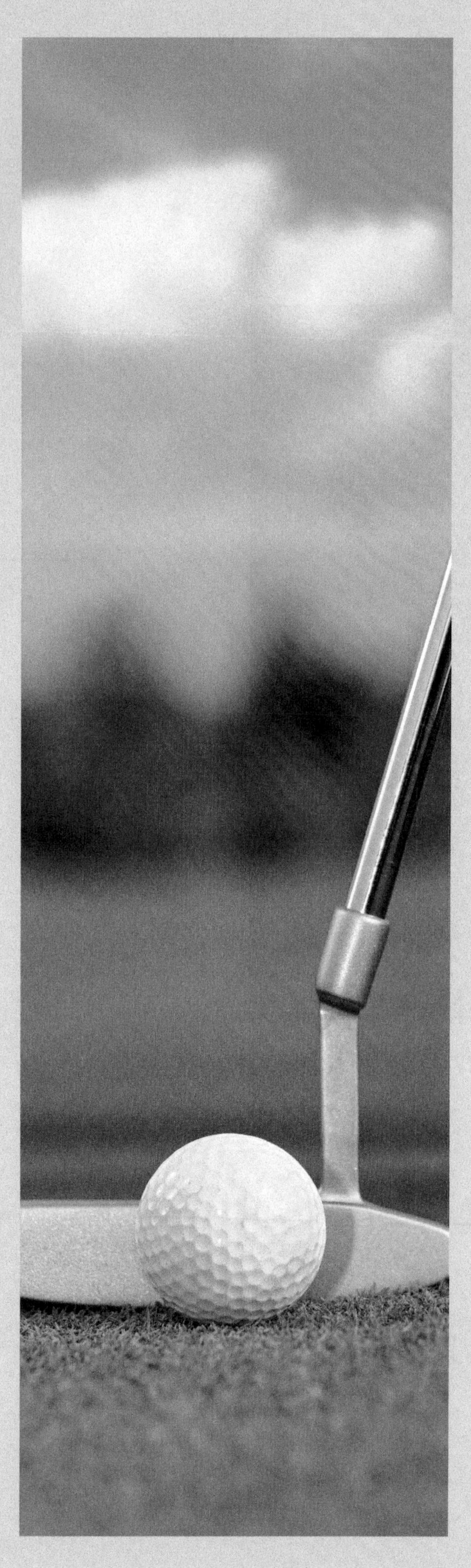

"I bought a self-correcting driver. Now it just yells at me every time I swing."

"My doctor told me to walk at least 2 miles a day. I said, 'Golf counts, right?'"

"I think I need a bigger golf bag. Not for more clubs, but for all the excuses I carry around."

"My golf game is like a box of chocolates. You never know what you're gonna get."

Finally figured out how to break 100 on the course. I switched to mini-golf.

Just bought a set of used clubs from a magician. Every time I swing, the ball disappears!

"Golf is a matter of confidence.
If you think you cannot do it,
there's no chance you will."

HENRY COTTON

Printed in Great Britain
by Amazon